PAPERS ON PRESIDENTIAL DISABILITY and the TWENTY-FIFTH AMENDMENT

by Dr. Kenneth Crispell
and other Medical, Legal,
and Political Authorities

Volume I

Edited by
KENNETH W. THOMPSON

Funded by the W. Alton Jones Foundation

UNIVERSITY
PRESS OF
AMERICA

Lanham • New York • Oxford

The Miller Center

University of Virginia

Copyright © 1997 by
University Press of America,® Inc.
4720 Boston Way
Lanham, Maryland 20706

12 Hid's Copse Rd.
Cummor Hill, Oxford OX2 9JJ

Copublished by arrangement with
The Miller Center of Public Affairs,
University of Virginia

The views expressed by the author(s) of this publication do not necessarily represent the opinions of the Miller Center. We hold to Jefferson's dictum that: "Truth is the proper and sufficient antagonist to error, and has nothing to fear from the conflict, unless by human interposition, disarmed of her natural weapons, free argument and debate."

Library of Congress Cataloging-in-Publication Data
(Revised for vol. 4)

Papers on presidential disability and the Twenty-fifth Amendment.
p. cm.
1. Presidents--United States--Succession. 2. United States--Constitutional
law--Amendments--25th. I. Thompson, Kenneth W. II.
KF5082.P37   1996
342.73'062--dc20   347.30262   88-1602 CIP

ISBN: 0-7618-0724-1 (v. 4: cloth: alk. ppr.)
ISBN: 0-7618-0725-X (v. 4: pbk: alk. ppr.)

TO

DR. KENNETH CRISPELL

Contents

CONTENTS

Preface

For any project, the beginning is often the measure of the future. The beginnings of the Miller Center's program on presidential disability go back to a meeting in Washington on 10 October 1985. In this fourth volume of papers on presidential disability we return to the origins of the study. Under the leadership of Dr. Kenneth Crispell, formerly vice president and dean for Health Services at the University of Virginia, the Center assembled a group of distinguished medical scientists, legal scholars, and social scientists to discuss the formation of a commission. Dr. Crispell had approached most of them individually, and the meeting was intended to build on his earlier discussions and research.

The Miller Center of Public Affairs of the University of Virginia has a twofold mandate: to seek understanding of the American presidency through study and research and to foster the improvement of the presidency. Specifically, the Center has sought to further the understanding of the presidency through the valued contributions of scholars in residence conducting research at the Center. In public affairs, the Center's main instrumentality for advancing ideas on the improvement of the presidency has been a series of seven national commissions whose membership has comprised public figures and professional staff from the University of Virginia.

The Miller Center Commission on Presidential Disability and the Twenty-fifth Amendment was the fourth of the national commissions organized by the Center, preceded by commissions on the presidential press conference, the nominating process, and presidential transitions. Co-chairmen of the commission were the two principal authors of the Twenty-fifth Amendment: the Honorable Herbert Brownell, who served as attorney general in the Eisenhower administration, and former Senator Birch Bayh of Indiana. Its recommendations were drafted by former *Washington*

Post Washington correspondent Chalmers M. Roberts. The Commission's vice-chairman was the Honorable Mortimer Caplin, director of the Internal Revenue Service in the Kennedy administration.

The commission's studies were staffed and administered by University of Virginia faculty. Professionals at the University who are qualified in the subject matter of the commission prepared papers which were made available to members of the commission. The authors of the papers also presented them to an audience of the wider University community and Miller Center family in forums and Rotunda lectures.

Introduction

The present volume begins with the text of the pre-commission meeting that led to the creation of a Miller Center Commission on Presidential Disability. The group who met in Washington on 10 October 1985 were convened to advise the Center on the need for and feasibility of a study of presidential disability. At a time somewhat past the midpoint of the Reagan administration, the conferees directed their attention to the experience of Dr. Dan Ruge, presidential physician in President Reagan's first term. His views were to provide a benchmark for many of the deliberations to follow. Dr. Ruge was unusually candid about his duties in what he referred to as a blue-collar job in the White House. He talked about the attempted assassination of the President two months into the administration. The account traces what happened from the shooting to the race to the hospital to Dr. Ruge's meeting with the vice president and the Cabinet to the President's release from the hospital. Curiously, Dr. Ruge had not met the vice president, who plays a vital role in the procedures of the Twenty-fifth Amendment, before that meeting. Dr. Ruge reviews the history of presidential physicians going back to President Andrew Jackson and the role of the physician in various presidencies and their rankings within the White House table of organization. He describes Reagan's remarkable conduct as a patient. His own optimistic attitude mirrored that of the President.

Much of the discussion centers on the Twenty-fifth Amendment, especially sections three and four. More than was true of the Brownell-Bayh commission that resulted from the pre-commission meeting, those who met in October 1985 tended to favor an advisory body made up of three physicians or one physician and two nonphysicians who would rule on the president's disability. Despite Dr. Ruge's reference to a blue-collar job, he maintained a rather effective relationship with the President. He discusses how he was selected, traveling with the President, the president's role, military versus civilian physicians, the workload, the president's right to pick his own physician, the presidential physician's use of other doctors, the letter that temporarily transfers power, the physician's response to immediate problems, his limited authority, and other issues. Dean Norman Knorr of the University of Virginia medical school discussed possible mental as distinct from physical incapacity. The group talked about particular presidents and health—for example, President Johnson. They hoped to approach various presidential physicians and solicit their views. Finally, they considered the role of the vice president in the process.

The second chapter in the book is a *tour d'horizon* of the various questions and principles to emerge from the 10 October 1985 meeting. Questions are raised and brought into sharper focus than was possible in the larger meeting. Basically, the group was comprised of medical and legal authorities. It would be a fair description of the pre-commission document and the summary to call them the "Articles of Confederation" for the Commission. The ideas provided the building blocks on which the commission's later work was based. They gave impetus to the launching of the commission simply because of the quality of the medical and legal people who led the discussion. In a memorandum of 5 November 1985, Professor Daniel J. Meador elaborated further on key questions that had been raised in the 1985 meeting and in the summary of discussions.

The third chapter derives from a meeting that took place on 14 February 1986 about four months later than the pre-commission meeting. The medical advisory group came together again in Washington and explored the following questions:

I.   The role of the president's physician;
II.   Possible guidelines for invoking Section 3;
III. The possibility and method of guaranteeing a medical input into the decision process;
IV.   Analysis of "Inability to Serve" in terms of physical or medical incompetence;
V.   References to Section 4;

VI. Conclusion: Any decision to use or not use medical information will inevitably be political.

The first substantive proposal for a commission on presidential disability grew out of the aforementioned conferences. Throughout, Dr. Kenneth Crispell, with the assistance of Dr. Carlos Gomez, was a key actor. The proposal raises some of the questions that the Miller Center Commission subsequently explored. The commission as finally constituted, however, appeared less concerned that various aspects of the amendment were fraught with problems. The proposal tends to reflect the understandable concern of medical authorities with the vagaries and imprecision of the political process. They are convinced that the presidential physician has "the keenest insight" into health problems. They are uncomfortable with the "inability to serve" clause in the amendment. They are most concerned, however, with who controls the U.S. nuclear arsenal if there is delay or ambiguity in the transfer of power ("Who has the suitcase?"). The proposal reviews the actions and chronology of the attempted Reagan assassination.

What becomes clear in comparing the two bodies is that the draft proposal asked more than the Center's commission could fulfill. The commission tended to accept the notion that the most one could hope was that the parties directly involved, especially the vice president, would use common sense. The Miller Center Commission trusted in the process of the Twenty-fifth Amendment. The doctors wanted more. Therefore, the list of questions is a valuable part of the study proposal. It points to the need for further study.

Section II is devoted to articles on the presidential physicians. Chapter 5 under Section II provides an overview of the relation of the presidential physician to the president. The physician faces two choices in the event of presidential disability: revealing the disability and setting in motion the procedures for his removal or participating in a cover-up. Three famous cases of cover-up are often cited: those of James Garfield, Woodrow Wilson, and Franklin D. Roosevelt. A central issue is how to define and determine "inability to serve." President Truman proposed a Committee of Seven drawn from the branches of government. The committee would choose a medical board that would present their findings on the president's health and make recommendations to the Committee of Seven, which would communicate with Congress. The board would distinguish between temporary and long-term disability. Others have made proposals, notably the late attorney general, Herbert Brownell. He suggested a written protocol involving the president, vice president, and presidential physician. Senator Birch Bayh pointed out that the problem of disability goes well beyond threats or acts of assassination. It involves health problems that are often far removed from public scrutiny. A final point in the paper deals with sedation and the ability to make decisions, such as in the Iran-contra affair.

The gravity of the problem of presidential disability is underscored by Dr. Hugh L'Etang, who in 1969 observed that in the past 60 years, six of ten American presidents and eleven of Britain's thirteen presidents had suffered incapacitating illnesses. This reference introduces the sixth chapter in the volume. Too often, illnesses in the White House are kept from the public. The classic case is Woodrow Wilson, but Franklin D. Roosevelt's health was, if anything, more troubling. Physicians were able to conceal and cover up presidential illnesses. Prior to the Twenty-fifth Amendment, aides to presidents dealt with the problem by executing voluntary agreements enabling a high official to declare the president's inability to serve. Where the president was unable to make the determination, the vice president, after "appropriate consultation," would do so. In either instance, the vice president would serve as acting president until the president resumed the powers and duties of office. President Kennedy specified that the Cabinet was the appropriate body he should consult, and President Johnson turned to House Speaker McCormick and later Vice President Humphrey. Prior to Kennedy, announcement of inability to serve took the form of agreements based on an exchange of letter. Dr. Crispell suggests other questions worthy of study, including the role of the White House staff in general and in connection with President Reagan's cancer surgery and the debate over whether or not to invoke the Twenty-fifth Amendment.

Chapter 7 provides a lively discussion of the precarious role of the president's physician by a respected *Washington Post* journalist,

Bill McAllister.   He begins by noting that the ranking of the presidential physician is 54 among 55 Reagan White House officials listed in the 1981 *Congressional Directory*. He also observes that the President in seven years has had four physicians.   Clearly, the position has low prestige both in the White House and the medical community.   McAllister discusses the work of the Miller Center Commission.   He notes that the commission rejected the proposal (made in pre-commission discussions) that the physician be subject to congressional approval.   He discusses the dual loyalty problem—to the patient and to the country—and the issue of confidentiality.   He suggests that someday some of these issues are likely to surface in presidential campaigns.   The issue of cronyism in the choice of presidential physicians receives attention, as does the question of military versus civilian doctors in the job.   The nature of the presidential physician's role means that he is likely to be more effective if he is a generalist in medicine, but a seasoned one.   Dr. Crispell has written about the need for a doctor who can diagnose an illness quickly and then assign specialists to care for the president's particular problem.   President Bush's physician, Dr. Burton Lee III, has written about this organizational question. The physician's *forte* should be his or her judgment. McAllister moves back and forth in discussing the Miller Center's findings and discussing information contained in Dr. Edward B. MacMahon's book, *Medical Cover-ups in the White House.*

An important part of the preparatory work for the Miller Center Commission on Presidential Disability took the form of interviews and correspondence with prominent medical, legal, and political personalities. This approach produced a significant amount of material that later proved valuable to the Commission.   For example, on 12 March 1985 Professor Meador interviewed Attorney General Meese. Apparently, no thought was given to invoking the Twenty-fifth Amendment when the President was shot.   Meese's concept regarding later use was that law enforcement and national defense had to coordinate in the event of another assassination attempt. Attorney General Smith and the defense secretary would have to judge whether a shooting was part of a general attack against the government. Mr. Meese said that President Reagan was fully able to sign bills the day after his surgery.   Hence, there was no need to invoke the Twenty-fifth Amendment. He saw no serious problem with the vice president being a key player in the decision process.

Professor Meador also interviewed Senator Hugh Scott (R-Pa.), which is the second item under Chapter 8. Meador sought advice on persons to consult regarding the commission, possible members, and ideas about changes in the present legal arrangements. Senator Scott suggested contacting senators such as Strom Thurmond, Mac Mathias, and Joe Biden; media figures, including Roger Mudd and Hugh Sidey; White House officials Philip Buchen and George Reedy; and Congressmen Richard Bolling and Barber Conable.

On behalf of Dr. Crispell, Lehman Ford interviewed Dr. Larry Altman of the *New York Times*. Dr. Altman responded to questions regarding confidentiality requested by "Very Important Persons" (VIPs) and their use of aliases. Altman considers this "arguably fraudulent." Among Twenty-fifth Amendment issues discussed by Dr. Altman are: psychiatric illnesses; 21-day maximum limit for Congress to decide on a presidential/vice presidential disagreement or presidential disability; and procedures for military command succession during presidential disability. Some favor a bifurcation of presidential power so that military command would devolve during a presidential disability crisis. Isn't this already provided for? Congress set aside consideration of this issue because it could deal with only so many issues at a time. Dr. Altman was helpful and expressed himself forcefully on various issues.

Dr. Crispell's interview with Dr. Dan Ruge follows. Crispell reviews with President Reagan's presidential physician such issues as competing interpretations of the treatment of Reagan after the shooting, the embargoing by Richard Darman of the Fielding procedural document at the time of the crisis, and Dr. Ruge's relationship with the Cabinet and vice president before the assassination attempt and his meeting with the Cabinet. Dr. Crispell also interviewed Senator Bayh and prepared a memorandum on Bayh's views on the disability process and the main issues the commission must discuss. Professor Meador also interviews Fred Fielding, counsel to President Reagan on 7 January 1985.

Chapter 9 contains correspondence between Fred Fielding, a graduate of the University of Virginia Law School who was counsel to President Reagan at the time of his exchange of letters with Professor Meador. Meador had raised the question of the administration's failure to invoke the Twenty-fifth Amendment subsequent to the President's cancer surgery. Mr. Fielding disclosed that prior to the surgery, his office did a review of the legislative history of the Twenty-fifth Amendment. He explains that the President had decided that a transfer of authority to the vice president was required. However, the letter was drafted in such a way that no precedent was established of invoking the Twenty-fifth Amendment for "future brief periods of disability." Counsel Fielding kindly provided some of the documentation that explains the basis for the decision by President Reagan. Also included is Counsel Fielding's response to Professor Meador's original inquiry on the subject of transfer of authority during the President's surgery.

The next chapter contains a series of memoranda and reports on presidential disability and the Twenty-fifth Amendment. They are examples of the preparation and special studies that antedated the work of the commission. Perhaps most significant is the memorandum reporting on the interview Dr. Carlos Gomez conducted with Mr. Lawrence Conrad, chief of staff to Senator Bayh's committee on the Twenty-fifth Amendment. The memorandum is important because if foreshadows the differences that emerged between the thinking of the medical group who spearheaded the move for a commission and the commission as it was finally constituted. First, Conrad traces the successful transitions undertaken under the amendment for the legal and constitutional transfer of powers. He mentions replacement of Agnew as vice president by Gerald Ford, Ford's replacement of Nixon as president, and Rockefeller's replacement of Ford as vice president. A line of succession was established. Where presidential illness is involved, other problems appear. What stands out in Dr. Gomez's memorandum is that problems that concern the medical group are of less moment to political operatives. Conrad was less concerned about the role of the vice president in the process, the nuclear code and who has it, the question of "inability to serve," a board of medical advisers, and rewriting the amendment. In fact, Conrad's view mirrors the views of the majority of the Miller Center Commission.

Chapter 11 is the report of the preliminary meeting of the presidential disability study group on 14 December 1984. Chapter 12 is Professor Meador's memo to colleague Paul Stephen on Section III in the amendment. His memo completes the volume.

Appendix A is a copy of the Eisenhower-Nixon agreement on the transfer of power dated 3 March 1958. Such agreement antedated the enactment and ratification of the Twenty-fifth Amendment.

Appendix B is a copy of the disability agreement between President John F. Kennedy and Vice President Johnson describing criteria for the transfer of power. This agreement provided the basis for a similar agreement between President Johnson and Vice President Humphrey.

Appendix C contains the text of a letter from President Reagan to the president pro tempore of the Senate and to the Speaker of the House notifying them that Vice President Bush would temporarily discharge the powers and duties of the President.

Appendix D is an excerpt from Barbara Bush's biography, *Barbara Bush: A Memoir,* that describes a meeting held in the Oval Office during the early days of George Bush's presidency to discuss the Twenty-fifth Amendment and what should be done if it became necessary to invoke that amendment.

I.

FORMING A COMMISSION: THE ORIGINS

CHAPTER ONE

Pre-Commission Meeting on the Twenty-Fifth Amendment[*]

KENNETH R. CRISPELL, M.D., EDITOR

DR. CRISPELL: Does everyone know what everyone else does? Dan Meador is a professor of constitutional law at the University of Virginia; Ken Thompson runs the White Burkett Miller Center for the Study of the Presidency; Tom Connally is one of our graduates who practices medicine in Washington and takes care of people in government; Dr. Dan Ruge was the President's physician in Mr. Reagan's first term; John Hogness is president of the Association of Academic Health Center; Monty DuVal chairs the American Health Care Institute that controls approximately one-quarter of America's voluntary not-for-profit beds; Norm Knorr is our dean at the University of Virginia; Roy Schwarz is assistant executive vice president of AMA, and was dean at Colorado; Bland Cannon was professor of neurosurgery at the University of Tennessee and was very active both in the AMA and the AMC; and

---

[*]*The Pre-Commission Meeting on the Twenty-Fifth Amendment was held in Washington, D.C. on 10 October 1985. Participants at the meeting include Dr. Kenneth Crispell, Dr. Bland Cannon, Dr. Merlin K. DuVal, Dr. Roy Schwarz, Dr. Tom Connally, Dr. John Hogness, Dr. Dan Ruge, Dr. Norman J. Knorr, Professor Kenneth W. Thompson, Professor Daniel Meador, Professor Paul Stephan, Mr. Reed Davis, and Mr. Wistar Morris.*

Paul Stephan is a professor at the University of Virginia Law School.

Dr. Ruge, I wonder if you would tell us in any way you wish on what happened during the shooting and what your involvement was or what your involvement was not.

DR. RUGE: This occurred about two months into the administration. I think if we had heard any shots the first week or two, we would not have been surprised, but having been to the Hilton at least five or six times in that two-plus months, we were all rather relaxed, and we walked out of the building, and there were the shots. There was no question that they were shots, and I was very close to the scene. I saw that there were three people lying on the ground. The President had on a brand-new dark pinstriped suit that day, which I think he was wearing for the first time. I didn't see a black pinstriped suit on the ground, and I realized that he hadn't been shot. About that time his limousine pulled away, and I realized that I had to go too, so I ran to my car, which was just beginning to move, and they stopped and picked me up and we had a fast ride down Connecticut Avenue. Fortunately, the police and everyone else were aware of the schedule and that the President would be returning to the White House, so Connecticut Avenue was completely cleared. I think we drove down it 60 miles an hour at least. I often wondered why Pennsylvania Avenue was cleared, but it finally dawned on me that the reason was because police were blocking traffic at Pennsylvania Avenue so that we could cross Pennsylvania Avenue to go to the White House. Westbound traffic on Pennsylvania Avenue was really nonexistent because it was being held back.

On the morning of that particular day, Jerry Parr, who was the senior agent in the presidential protective division and I, still being rather new, had a chat about what would we do if something happened today, and we picked George Washington University, which is the hospital we always pick if something takes place in this part of town. It was in the ride down that Jerry Parr saw blood on the President's lips and decided that we were going to go to George Washington Hospital. We got to the hospital, and the President's car actually pulled up to the hospital ahead of mine because the rest of us had to go around the circle; I don't think his car did. He walked in, slumped, and was picked up and taken to the emergency room. Thanks to that very active and very responsive hospital—and I would say particularly to Dr. Joe Giordano, who is a surgeon here in town—the care at this hospital was fabulous. We did not know that the President had been shot. There was no blood; his brand-new suit looked perfectly OK, but when they cut it off of him, we saw just a little bit of blood on his shirt in the left axilla. After it (the shirt) was cut off, we saw a very small laceration. By this time he was really dyspneic, and my thought was that he had had a coronary before we saw evidence of a wound. Then we realized there was a wound and obviously a severe one because he was very short of breath. But I have to tell you that I don't think the man was ever in great danger because of the speed in which everything was done. I stayed out of the way and at the foot of the bed. One of the first things that we did was take off his shoes and socks. I felt the dorsalis pedis pulse, and it never disappeared. I had heard stories of his being in deep shock, and I think they were greatly exaggerated.

Giordano and I spoke to Dr. Aaron, who was the thoracic surgeon. A chest tube had been placed, and a lot of blood was removed from his chest. At 3:30 p.m. he was in the operating room and the operation was underway. I would say it was a very straightforward operation made difficult because the bullet was flattened, because it hit the limousine, ricocheted, and entered his chest. So it was actually difficult to find, but it was finally found and removed. That was fortunate because it was a lead azide bullet. In the case of Delahante the cop, I think his operation actually took place because they found out it was a lead azide bullet. Of course, they had the bullet of Tim McCarthy, the agent, who was in rather good condition.

I think the operation was done very well, very promptly, and he was taken to the recovery room, which is on the same floor at about 6:00 p.m. By this time, Lyn Nofziger had moved in as the White House press man since Jim Brady, who was the press secretary, had been shot. I met Nofziger and a few other people in Dennis O'Leary's office (Dennis O'Leary is the dean for clinical services at GW), and we had a discussion about who should be talking to the press, and I think they had already made up their minds that it should be Dennis. When I was asked, I said by all means the hospital should do the speaking because he was really a patient of the hospital, he was not my patient. We very amicably decided that Dennis O'Leary should be the spokesman, which he was and did a very good job.

I didn't know exactly what my job was, so I just stuck around, and I was in the recovery room practically the entire night. I did have a room in the hospital. I had a White House telephone. It didn't take the White House communications agency very long to do all these things. I had my own phone, but I doubt that I was in my room more than 40 minutes that night.

I think you've all heard the stories about one-liners, and most of those were written in papers and magazines. The President is the kind of person who could entertain the people who were taking care of him. He's just a prince of a guy in many ways, and in that way in particular. I think that we felt at about 2:30 in the morning that everything was coming along very well. From that time on, everything really looked very good, and I think that was about the first time that I realized or had time to think about the fact that we had had a sick man.

The next morning we decided to move him into the intensive care unit. Sometime during the early morning hours, I don't know exactly when, I was asked to be at the White House at about 7:30 a.m. to speak to the staff. This invitation came from Jim Baker, who was the chief of staff.

DR. CRISPELL: Who asked you, Dan?

DR. RUGE: That I'm not certain of. I'm told that Jim Baker asked me, but I don't think he asked me in person. I think the message was probably given to me. I did go home when I knew that I was going to be doing this to put on some decent clothes, and at 7:30 a.m. I met the members of the staff in the Roosevelt Room where they have their staff meetings. That usually does not include the physician. It was also the first time that I ever met George Bush face-to-face, although we had had telephone conversations. Bush asked me if I would be available at 8:30 a.m. to speak to the

6

Cabinet. I said of course I would. Then the second press conference started in the Old Executive Office Building at about 8:00 a.m., and Dennis O'Leary and I appeared on the stage. It was understood that I was there so the people could see me. The fact that I was there meant that I wasn't at the hospital. Also, there was no plan for me to take any of the questions, and it was sort of agreed upon that somebody would get me out at about 8:30 a.m. or a little before that time so I could leave and go to the Cabinet room and talk to the Cabinet. I know that Tip O'Neill was there also. I told them the good news as I had told the staff an hour earlier. I think that morning, he signed his first bill.

During the night, he asked a question about other people involved, and we ignored his question because for one thing he still had an endotracheal tube. I thought he would get emotional if he heard about Jim Brady, so we ignored the question. During the meeting of the Cabinet another person who was there was Paul Laxalt, and he and I had a chat. He said you had better tell the President about Jim Brady as fast as you can because he'll be upset if he finds out from someone else. I went back to the hospital in the vice president's motorcade. By that time Nancy was at the hospital too, and I told her we had to tell her husband about Jim Brady. She asked who was going to do it, and I said, "I am." She said, "I'd like to go with you," so she did. We told him, and he was very upset and actually quite tearful. At this time, he was in the intensive care unit on one of the upper floors. The physicians in the intensive care unit thought we were a bit of a problem because there were all these people. They said that he was really good enough to be out of the intensive care unit, so we agreed that he should be moved.

About this time there was some discussion about whether to stay here or go to Bethesda. I don't really know who raised the question, but I think it came from the Secret Service. It was agreed that we stay here. We had to find some space and discussed what should be closed off and so forth. I think we got about eight or ten rooms in one wing, and I had a room. A separate room was prepared for the President. They put bullet-proof glass in the window and painted the room. So at about 5:00 or 6:00 p.m., we moved down there. The room reeked of paint, so we moved him into a room that didn't have the bullet-proof glass. He actually started to see one or two people. I think I remember Governor Connally the best. I had never seen him before. He came when the President was having a nap at 10:00 the next morning, and I told him, "The President would like to see you, but he is taking a nap." He said, "Well, that's all right, I don't mind waiting." A little later he asked me if the President had awakened yet. I said, "No, he hasn't." He said, "Well, I really don't have to see him. Why don't you just tell him I was here." I said, "No, I think you ought to stick around because he'll be upset if he doesn't get to see you. You'll be out there on the street and the press will ask you had you seen the President, and you'll have to say, "No, he was asleep!" He said, "Well, I wouldn't have to say that." In other words, he would have been willing to lie.

DR. CRISPELL: I can't remember, where was Connally shot? In the shoulder?

DR. RUGE: He was shot in the hand, for one place.

DR. CRISPELL: So he had been through it.

DR. RUGE: Yes, and he is a very good visitor. I was in the next room, and he had a very good time, a short time. Vernon Jordan, who had also been shot, came later. Well, things really went very well. I think that like everyone else who had been shot in one of the body cavities, he ran a temperature. But presidents aren't supposed to have fevers. This was one heck of a big deal. I decided I wasn't going to give any numbers because if you tell these clowns that his temperature is 98.0 yesterday and it was 98.2 today, they would wonder what went wrong. I think this was sort of the beginning of my being accused of not telling everything.

I'm going to backtrack a little bit. Before I actually went over there, I did deliberately give some interviews, and one of the interviews stated that I didn't think it was necessary to tell them every time about the President's health. People have remembered that statement. I don't think it is everyone's business to know. The main reason I wanted some publicity was that when I was asked to

8

take the job, I wanted people to know why I got the job. It's very simple. Mrs. Reagan's father and I were partners for many years, and we maintained a friendship. He's the guy who picked me. I didn't want this to be discovered sometime later as nepotism or whatever you want to call it.

The President's health is everyone's business. Bill Lukash and I talked about that once before. He was my predecessor and had been at the White House for 14 years and had been the physician for both Ford and Carter. We had a conversation, and he said that what people really have to know is if he is in good health or not in good health, whether he is able to serve or isn't able to serve, and that's really all people have to know. I think that is putting it correctly. At least that's what I wanted to remember him saying. I thought to myself that it had worked pretty well for him for 14 years and that was how I was going to do it too. I think all you can say is that the President had a very fine convalescence with a fever. He had lost a lot of blood. He had a lot of transfusions the afternoon of the shooting, and fortunately he did not get hepatitis. The hospital had a list of all of the donors, and they were all checked for viral hepatitis. He was shot on Monday, and he went to that room on Tuesday. I think we delayed having a picture until Thursday, and the argument of the press was, well, he has his picture in the paper every day when he's well. We should have a picture now too. I could understand that, but I don't agree. It was decided that we had better get a picture before people started to wonder, so we had a picture. There is a picture of the President and Nancy walking down the hall. The people saw that he was up and walking. I don't think we had to have another picture.

We entered on Monday, and the second Saturday after that he went home. Mrs. Reagan was very anxious to get him home, and she kept badgering me. I told her that he could go home either Saturday, Sunday, or Monday. She said OK, it's going to be Saturday. I said, "Well, if it's going to be Saturday, them I'm going to have to stay with you." She said that was all right. To make a long story short, I stayed in the Lincoln Room for two nights. We were still giving him some medicines.

I know that certain people seemed to be around an awful lot. I remember one time Strom Thurmond was talking to me, and I really didn't quite understand it. He asked me how *he* was doing, and I thought he was talking about the President, but he had Jim Brady in mind. I told him he was doing great and that he should be going home any day now. Strom Thurmond goes up to see Mrs. Brady and tells her how well Jim is doing and that he would be going home any day now. There were an awful lot of people who were around a good bit. He started being President on Tuesday, a day after the shooting.

DR. CRISPELL: Did anyone in the White House staff ask you what his long-term outlook was when you talked to the staff and the Cabinet?

DR. RUGE: No, but being the optimist that I am and realizing how well he was doing, I'm sure I said it. He was very good. For personal reasons, I was very interested in the welfare of Jerry Parr at that time. Jerry and I had become rather good friends, and I knew somewhere along the line that somebody was going to be wondering why the hell did you guys have him get shot. I made a point at that staff meeting and at the Cabinet meeting to tell them how wonderful Jerry Parr was and how his quick decision to go to the hospital and so forth saved the day. I never denied the fact that delays would have been disastrous because they would have been. But now I don't think that anyone really asked that question.

DR. CRISPELL: Do you think they ever asked O'Leary or the surgeon?

DR. RUGE: You mean the staff? I'm sure then didn't. As a matter of fact, most people saw very little of O'Leary or the surgeons, and it isn't that I wanted to deny these people the right to talk because that certainly was not my intent. I always sort of thought that my job was to see to it that physicians who were asked to take charge of the President would be free to take care of him as if he were any other patient. That's how I really viewed my job. I viewed it that way before I went over there; I did then, and I still do. These people have no idea how much I spared them. I spared O'Leary and I spared Ben Aaron from having to have many confrontations with Mrs. Reagan for one thing and with any of the people taking care of him. I thought this was what I owed them.

DR. CRISPELL: When you met with the staff at 7:30 a.m. after the shooting, did I understand you to say that they did not inquire, or you did not say what the President's condition was at that time?

DR. RUGE: Yes, I did; I told them it was excellent.

DR. CRISPELL: You described it?

DR. RUGE: Yes.

DR. CRISPELL: In detail, or just generally?

DR. RUGE: Well, in generalities. I told them this could have been a very serious thing, that it was a serious wound and because of Jerry Parr and the efficiency of the emergency room, he was in good condition. The emergency room and the recovery room were absolutely super.

DR. CRISPELL: But they were already alerted, weren't they?

DR. RUGE: They hadn't been alerted very much. I think the fact of the matter is that the reason he got along as well as he did is that they treated him the same way they would have treated you and me if we had been there.

DR. CRISPELL: Did anyone on the staff at that meeting ask you rather expressly whether you thought he was able to function as President, or words to that effect?

DR. RUGE: No, but I'm sure that somebody did sometime.

DR. CONNALLY: Did you give an opinion as to his ability to function?

DR. RUGE: I might have used those words, but I am sure that the optimism I conveyed would have told him that. The optimism on my part was not an act.

MR. MEADOR: The Cabinet meeting was an hour late. Did anybody in that meeting quiz you or press you about his ability to perform and function? No? Was the entire Cabinet present at that meeting?

DR. RUGE: I don't know if everybody was there.

MR. MEADOR: But most of them were there?

DR. RUGE: Yes, I think most of them were there.

MR. MEADOR: I would like to go back to the day before. If these are inappropriate questions, just say so. To the best of your knowledge, did anyone accompanying the President on any trip ever carry with them a blank form of a letter addressed to the present pro tem of the Senate and Speaker of the House that the President could sign on a second's notice saying I'm unable to perform the duties of my office?

DR. RUGE: I have no knowledge of that.

MR. MEADOR: When he arrived at the hospital, did I understand you to say that he got out of his car and fainted?

DR. RUGE: He started to slump, and then he was picked up.

MR. MEADOR: Did he go unconscious?

DR. RUGE: No, I would say not.

MR. MEADOR: Did he regain consciousness before the surgery began?

DR. RUGE: Oh, he was conscious the whole time. As a matter of fact, he and I actually had some conversation in the emergency room.

MR. MEADOR: I suppose once you said, "We're going into surgery," he was sufficiently conscious and able to have signed a letter stating that he was unable to perform if he wanted to.

DR. RUGE: Oh, yes.

MR. MEADOR: Wasn't that the time he made the crack about hoping all the physicians and surgeons were Republicans?

DR. RUGE: That actually occurred in the operating room before he was operated on.

DR. CRISPELL: And he said, "Who's minding the store?" Is that the crack or not?

DR. RUGE: I think that happened afterward. As a matter of fact, I don't believe that happened until the next day.

MR. MEADOR: Once he went into surgery, what was the first point at which he regained consciousness sufficiently to carry on some sort of conversation?

DR. RUGE: The interesting thing is that there were conversations going on at 7:00, 8:00 p.m. Even with the tube, he was able to talk.

MR. MEADOR: Was he out of the recovery room by that time?

DR. RUGE: No, he was in the recovery room. He was in the recovery room until sometime after 6:00 or 7:00 a.m. on Tuesday.

MR. MEADOR: But he had regained consciousness the previous evening.

DR. RUGE: Oh yes. He didn't receive some medicines, and this, I think, should just stay in here. It was impossible to aspirate the bronchoscope through the tube because it had a kink in it, so there was a fair amount of secretion in the tube and it needed sucking. During this time he had to have some pain killers. He was alert about seven or eight o'clock that night. I was in the room, and Nancy and their son came in for about 20 minutes. He had some communication with them. A lot of these notes were written during that night, and I don't think that we really worried about him.

MR. THOMPSON: Was the consciousness the kind where one moves in and out of consciousness?

DR. RUGE: Yes, I think so.

MR. THOMPSON: So if he had been presented with something that required concentration, it would have been difficult.

MR. MEADOR: Did it ever cross your mind at anytime that night and into the early morning of the following day or did you ever hear anybody mention the idea of somehow invoking the Twenty-fifth Amendment?

DR. RUGE: No.

DR. CRISPELL: Didn't Vice President Bush call you by the wrong name?

DR. RUGE: Max Friedersdorf [Congressional Relations] and I have white hair. One day I was going up the stairway, and he was right behind me. He said, "Hi, Max." Then he saw it wasn't Max.

MR. MEADOR: Do you think that would be one small thing that could be done in the future to have a working familiarity with the vice president?

DR. RUGE: I think this is one of the things that should be talked about; namely, my perception of the job. I consider it a blue-collar

14

job, and I have said so, and I think other people like you should be aware that it is. The physician is one of the hired help. I don't want to do all the talking because I'm sure you have other things you would like to discuss here.

The presidents have always had doctors, and most of the time it was a loose relationship. I think they usually had doctors who lived in the neighborhood, and it was a very loose relationship. There was one doctor who attended every president from Jackson to Lincoln. Another doctor, Huntt [*sic*], attended five. I understand that he had an honorary M.D. from the University of Maryland. Then pretty soon some doctors used surgeon generals of the Army or Navy or in some instances their doctors became surgeon generals of the Army and Navy.

The first person to ever hold the title of physician to the president was a fellow by the name of Joel T. Boone, who attended Harding, Coolidge, and Hoover. Hoover created the position, physician to the president. When the physician to the president became a part of the military office, I don't really know. There is a thing in the White House called special support service to the president. At the present time the head of the special support service is a guy by the name of Ed Hickey who at the beginning of this administration was a deputy assistant to the president made into assistant to the president, and he will soon be going to something else. When this special support service meets, it includes me or the doctor, the head of what is called WHCA (White House Communications Agency), and they come from all of the services. There are just loads of them, and what they do is phenomenal. Every place I ever went I had my own phone—in China, in a Winnabago, in a trailer, in a hotel room—even if we were only going to be there for an afternoon. These phones are put in by these people in advance. So WHCA is very important in the special support services program. They obviously have a lot to do with all types of communication. Other people in there are the pilot of Air Force I. The number-one pilot of the helicopters is a Marine. The man at Camp David is Navy. The White House mess is Navy, but an ex-Navy who is now a civilian is in charge of the mess. There are five military aides—Army, Navy, Air Force, Marine, and Coast Guard.

15

DR. CRISPELL: Now, the military are not the football people.

DR. RUGE: Yes they are.

DR. CRISPELL: This is the football team.

DR. RUGE: That's one of those things that is incorrect about the interview. I think I wrote to you about it, so I think you have the right name. Somewhere you have the word that Joseph Muratti, a Secret Service agent had the football that day. It was Jose Muratti, the Army military aide.

DR. CRISPELL: He's a military aide.

DR. RUGE: He was the military aide that day, and he is the one who had the football that day.

DR. CRISPELL: But they meet when the President is going somewhere?

DR. RUGE: They're always along. The military aide and the physician are probably closer to the President physically than anybody else. Generally speaking, the physician is more so if for no other reason than he is the only one. Even when we had four physicians for the White House, I always took it upon myself to be the one because I did what I thought was my job. So my proximity physically was always very great. Then there are several spinoffs. Number one, I think it is rather awkward for a very healthy 70-year-old guy with dark hair and a good outlook to have a white-haired old doctor trudging along because you wonder what the hell's going to happen now. So I have always made myself as inconspicuous as possible. I did it because I assumed that he wanted it that way, and I was quite sure that the West Wing crowd would have resented too much exposure for me. You had that feeling, and I think it's the right feeling. I'm not really paranoid, I'm just sensitive. So the military aides are the closest after the physician.

People around the president think they are very important. Importance is related to when and where. It's much more

16

important if the President is in Honolulu, for example, than in Rockwell. I think the hour of the day enters into this a little bit. One time the President and Nancy and a Secret Service agent who was a military aide and I were the only ones in the helicopter. There had never been that few people in the helicopter before. Nancy asked everybody was, and I said, "Well, it's 11:30." I said to him, "You know, it really only takes five of us to run the country." He said, "And the pilot." That's an example of whether or not an assistant to the president rides up the hill or not. He might do it at 4:30 p.m., but at 11:30, it wasn't quite that important.

Another story is about an elevator in the State Capitol in Tennessee that holds only four people. The President used that elevator one time, and the other three people on it were a Secret Service agent, the military aide, and me. I have often wondered who would have been bumped if Nancy had been there. I suppose I would have been.

DR. CRISPELL: A military aide cannot be bumped by law.

DR. RUGE: Well, apparently not.

DR. CRISPELL: By national defense command, he cannot be bumped.

DR. RUGE: And according to the manifest, the doctor. There is a manifest for everything, even elevators. I sometimes ignored it because I was not about to get on an elevator that was already crowded. The President needs oxygen just as much as anyone else, and I have been on an elevator two or three times that had not functioned because there were too many people on it. There reason there were too many people on it was that people who were not on the manifest got on the elevator. So I made a point to be conspicuous by my absence if the elevator was crowded. On at least one occasion, I understand that the President sort of faked a chest pain and said, "Where's Dan, where's Dan." So he knew I was not where I should have been.

DR. CRISPELL: Had you read the Twenty-fifth Amendment and studied it?

DR. RUGE: Well, I could have recited the four parts to you at the time. I got acquainted with that as soon as I knew about it, and I carried it with me.

DR. CRISPELL: Had you met Fred Fielding?

DR. RUGE: By that time, no.

DR. CRISPELL: And he never called you during the time. He made out the letter on both occasions, if the press is right.

DR. RUGE: I did not know him at that time.

DR. CRISPELL: Is there any way we can tell where he got his information? Was it all from the staff? In other words, he did not ask anything medical during that time when he made it out.

DR. RUGE: Not from me.

MR. MEADOR: Was he present at that 7:30 a.m. staff meeting?

DR. RUGE: I don't know. I did not know him at that time.

MR. MEADOR: Were there many people at that 7:30 meeting?

DR. RUGE: I would say there were all of a dozen.

MR. MEADOR: Could you name the ones you do remember being present?

DR. RUGE: I'm not sure I could really name them all, but obviously Jim Baker and Bush were there, and I'm quite positive that Ed Meese was there. I did not know all of these people at that time. We had only been into this thing two months, and the physician had very little to do at this meeting.

18

MR. MEADOR: Was the vice president present again at the 8:30 Cabinet meeting? Was he presiding at that meeting?

DR. RUGE: Yes, and Al Haig was there.

DR. CRISPELL: Did anyone ask you or did they ask the surgeon following the surgery when the President would be capable of transacting business?

DR. RUGE: No one asked me. I think I told you, as I think I told them, I didn't use those words. I think if you had listened to me at 7:30 or 8:30 that morning, there would not be any doubt in your mind but that I was very optimistic.

DR. CRISPELL: Did you know that the President was signing bills?

DR. RUGE: Yes.

DR. CRISPELL: Would you want him to sign something that could change the country at that time?

DR. RUGE: He was really very alert.

MR. MEADOR: In connection with what he was signing?

DR. CRISPELL: When would you have made that decision?

DR. RUGE: I think as I told you I was quite convinced of that at about 2:30 a.m. That is about the time it dawned on me, "My god, this has been an important night."

MR. MEADOR: Well then, at about ten hours, you would have made that decision.

DR. DUVAL: Who else could have made the same decision that you did that he was competent to sign that piece of paper? Anyone who knew him?

DR. RUGE: I would think so.

MR. MEADOR: Suppose it is 7:30 a.m. on Tuesday. You go to the President and say we have just received word that Soviet army units crossed the Chinese border in sizeable strength. Would he had been in a position to deal with that situation and decide what would be the appropriate response?

DR. RUGE: I would have thought so, yes.

DR. CRISPELL: Was he on demerol?

DR. RUGE: He had a little morphine that night, but from the next morning on he had almost nothing except aspirin. There was a problem during the week, I forget what it was. In the middle of the week when he was running this fever, we were a little worried. He was actually febrile, and Dr. Aaron did a bronchoscopy. I told Dr. Aaron, "I can't tell you what the problem is, but it is very important that he not be sedated." He wasn't sedated; he was bronchoscoped, and some secretions were sucked out.

MR. MEADOR: If I can go along the same line of questioning, at the 8:30 a.m. Cabinet meeting, if the vice president had said, "We are to discuss whether to invoke the Twenty-fifth Amendment, and here are the papers prepared for him to sign if the majority of the Cabinet thinks that we should transfer authority to the vice president. We want your judgment. Do you think we should do this, or do you think the President is able to function," what would you have said to that question?

DR. RUGE: I would have said that he was able to function. I think you have to take my word that I would have also said that if they had asked me that question and if I had thought he was not able to function, I would have said that he wasn't able to function.

MR. MEADOR: Was there ever a time from that point on when he was not able to?

20

DR. CRISPELL: First of all, Dan, I appreciate your willingness to share how amazing the experience was. I have had morphine, and it makes you very euphoric. I would have given away the world. Wouldn't you have given away the world when you were on morphine?

DR. RUGE: No, I got vomiting as a complication of morphine!

DR. CRISPELL: My point is that I think judgment is blurred with any narcotics. Wouldn't you agree?

DR. RUGE: Yes, yes I would, and . . .

DR. CRISPELL: So he literally had minimal functional powers. The thing that amazes me with an open chest wound is the few times I have watched patients recover, it hurts even with medication like aspirin.

DR. RUGE: You have to know something about the President's stark physical attributes. I'm not saying that he has a low pain tolerance or anything like that. I'm just saying that here is a fellow who would probably have a great deal of pain and not tell anyone about it. As a matter of fact, it is all part of Ronald Reagan being president. Ronald Reagan is a great actor. He finally got an appropriate role in a play. I think, I remember another time, April 1982, when we had him in Bethesda for a urology workup. I happened to walk out with him. I actually have a very nice picture of the two of us together in which he is waving to the crowd. I heard Bill Plante say, "Gee, he really is an actor. Anybody who can have done what he's had done and come out here smiling like that is something." He knows what is expected. You almost never have to edit any of his pictures. He knows how to make it right the first time. Another thing he is able to do is—they do many of little recordings, such as 30-second, 55-second recordings, and so forth. He had to do five or six of those, one right after the other, and most of the time none of them are repeated. In other words, if he is supposed to say his message in 55 seconds, he says it in 55 seconds. Of course, it is written out that way. I think I have been

21

around him once or twice when one of the five or six had to be done over because the timing was not quite correct, and obviously he was reading it. Another thing is that he really appreciates people who are with him. This is a little bit of the acting business. If this were a holding room and he were to go out there in about two minutes to talk to about 2,000 people, he would be entertaining this crowd until about 15 seconds before he had to go out. That is the way he does it. I think he does it largely because he likes to do it. It is also sort of his way of saying, "It is nice of you to be here. I know that you would rather be doing something else." An actor can really carry that off well.

MR. THOMPSON: Could I ask a question and preface it by saying that Dean Rusk thought presidential health was a vital area we ought to look into when I was at Rockefeller Center. A week before John Foster Dulles died, Rusk had a long talk with him, and Dulles said, "If I had been well, I would not have handled certain policy questions as I did." The only hint Rusk got was that he did refer to Suez and Aswan. He said not so much that he would have made a different decision, but that the policy end of it would have been handled differently. So Rusk put both the medical staff at Rockefeller and others to work on this, as well as a couple of us in the social sciences. We talked to many people, and the medical people were sympathetic with doing more in this area in trying to find out what we should do, but we could never find a way to connect the health end to the inability to serve. In other words, the connection between policy and handling of policy and health was the slippery thing. We finally gave up on it. We commissioned a couple if historians to do something and then just threw up our hands. Rusk was in Charlottesville three or four days ago, and we talked about it again.

Are there limits to the role of the medical person's evaluation of ability to serve and is there any way on a joint basis that a medical man and a policy person could work together on this? You have not expected, I would suppose, or are in any position to be able to say, is he quite as sharp in the way he handles an outline on what he says to the Russians. If there was a Jim Baker available to

22

whom you were close, is that something where two people could work together?

DR. RUGE: Well, I'm going to say this. I think that the position should be used a little bit more than it has been, and it is one of my criticisms of the job. It is one of the reasons I call it a blue-collar job. I do not believe that a physician is consulted as much as he might be, although I have never had a problem like the one you were talking about. I had the feeling, however, that had there been such a problem, it would have been very difficult. That is in spite of the fact that if the President had not been in good condition at 7:30 or 8:30 the next morning, I would have not hesitated at all to have said so. I did at that time realize that we had had a problem during the night, and I would not have been afraid to have said that he isn't competent.

MR. MEADOR: Do you have any thoughts or ideas about some sort of supplemental or additional arrangements? There have been various suggestions going back into the 1960s before the Senate hearings about some sort of independent or outside group. For example, it has been suggested that some three physicians who are totally outside of the White House periodically examine the President or are on call to come in and give an independent evaluation. Do you have any ideas about whether any kind of mechanism like that would be desirable?

DR. RUGE: I think it would be all right. I certainly would not have quit the job if that had been done. I do believe that some of the suggestions have gone a bit far. I have heard most of them since I left the job because there has been quite a flap about the President's cancer in which I have gotten involved too. I think a president should have a right to select his own physician just as you have to select your physician. If he wants to take advice from his father-in-law, I don't object. He has that right too. I often wondered about competence and so forth, and I had my own notions on what I would do if I had a problem. I had done a five-year tour at the VA central office before I went to the White House, and I knew some very fine physicians, including neurologists and mental health people over there. I would have had access to them at any time, and it was my duty to always seek assistance.

MR. MEADOR: Would you have felt inhibited in any way by the physician/patient confidentiality in talking to other people? For example, going to the staff in the White House and saying, "Look, the President's in bad shape right now; you probably don't know it, but he's got thus and so," or telling that to the Cabinet or the vice president?

DR. RUGE: I don't think that I would have been inhibited.

MR. MEADOR: You wouldn't have felt that there would be a breech of the physician/patient relationship?

DR. RUGE: Well, I would have told him the same thing. I would have told him and her what I would have told you.

MR. MEADOR: You would have communicated this totally?

DR. RUGE: Yes, I would have told him for sure and probably her too.

MR. THOMPSON: What if they had said, don't carry this any further?

DR. RUGE: I would have done it anyhow.

DR. CONNALLY: Would you think it would be helpful from day one from the day you assumed the position to the President to sit down and have that understanding with him and say, "Mr. President, the physician/patient confidentiality is terribly important, but your reputation and the running of the country is so important that I have a responsibility"?

DR. RUGE: Absolutely.

DR. CONNALLY: I took care of a judge who was impaired for some time. I desperately wish I had done that ahead of time.

DR. SCHWARZ: I want to ask two or three things. I'm assuming that President Reagan is your boss.

DR. RUGE: Yes, ultimately, yes.

DR. SCHWARZ: If you were going to be dismissed, he would have to at least concur with that judgment.

DR. RUGE: I have a certificate that says I serve at his pleasure.

DR. DUVAL: You are also his personal physician, is that accurate?

DR. RUGE: The title is physician to the president. I was his personal physician, yes.

DR. DUVAL: He didn't have anyone else that he saw when he had a runny nose, hemorrhoids, or anything like that?

DR. RUGE: No.

DR. DUVAL: I gather from what you said that you were never placed in a position where you were asked, or it was implied, that it would be better if you obscured or withheld or it would not be timely to do it at 9:00 o'clock versus 11:00.

DR. RUGE: No, I was never asked anything. I was never asked to do anything that I thought in any way curtailed me in doing what I thought I should do. I think I can answer that this really never happened, but I want to talk a little about the summer and a few things that have happened since.

DR. DUVAL: Let me ask one more question. In your experience, was there ever a time in which a medical decision was made primarily on political grounds and not on medical grounds?

DR. RUGE: The answer is that it never happened. I do want to make a few comments about the summer. Stu Spencer, who was the campaign manager, made the statement that there was no politics in the polyp. I don't know if you read that, but that is a cute quote. My wife thought it was cute, and I did too, and I said it was a damn lie.

MR. MEADOR: Back to his surgery, the President did invoke the Twenty-fifth Amendment for the brief period of time he was in the operating room, I gather.

DR. CRISPELL: No, not officially. He said he was not invoking the Twenty-fifth Amendment. It's in the letter.

MR. MEADOR: Let me lay that aside for a moment. For the purpose of this discussion, assume that the letter could be construed as invoking the Twenty-fifth Amendment. Do you think it was appropriate to invoke the Twenty-fifth Amendment for this surgery this past summer or not? If you had been the White House physician at that time and your advice had been sought, what would you have said?

DR. RUGE: I would have told him to use it.

MR. MEADOR: Now why would you have told him to use it then and not in the shooting incident?

DR. RUGE: My guess is, and this is inferred, that people in 1981 like Darman were thinking about invoking it, weren't they? Five years on the job is different than two months, and in 1985 there was no urgency. In 1981, after the shooting, things moved too fast.

DR. CRISPELL: Fielding [counsel to the President] had the papers ready to go at the time.

DR. RUGE: It was discussed. There is a big difference between Dan Ruge on 30 March 1981 after a shooting when he had only been on the job two months for one thing and what Dan Ruge

26

would have been like four years later when he would have actually had time from April 1981 to July 1985 to think about it. I think very honestly in 1981 because of the speed of everything and the fact that we had a very sick person that the Twenty-fifth Amendment would never have entered my mind even though I probably had it in my little black bag. I carried it with me. The Twenty-fifth Amendment never occurred to me.

MR. MEADOR: Do you think it would have occurred to you if the shooting had happened four years later?

DR. RUGE: Yes.

MR. MEADOR: After the President recovered, did he at any time ask why Section 4 of the Twenty-fifth Amendment wasn't used and why didn't someone move on that after he was shot?

DR. RUGE: If that kind of conversation ever occurred, I never heard about it, and I think that this is somewhat indicative of where the White House places the importance of the position of physician to the president. I don't think they consider it a very important job.

MR. THOMPSON: Would you explain the issue that James Reston raised in a column where he said—not the one on the Twenty-fifth, but on an earlier occasion—that someone ought to have cautioned the presidents about excessive travel after some things were discovered? He said speeches and all of these trips were an unnecessary strain for a 70-year-old man who had had some surgery and gone through what he had gone through.

DR. RUGE: I wasn't there anymore, but I am pretty sure that discussions like that might have taken place. I'm a little bit annoyed with the present physicians at the White House because I don't think they have kept me informed the way I used to keep all of the President's physicians informed. I had a very good relationship with an allergist, a urologist, and an internist in California. I kept in touch with them. As a matter of fact, all three of them saw him during my time over there. They saw him a number of times in

27

California and at the White House. My successor is the one who was the urologist. After that horrible article about me in the *Washington Post* and my opinion of it, it would have been more courteous to have kept people informed.

I'm quite positive that by April 1985 the President had been told that more had to be done. As a matter of fact, I know that. His decision to go to Bitburg was his. I don't think that anyone told him that he should not, but he knew then that he was going to have to have more done. I think that at least some of the delays were his idea, and another thing I think you have to remember is that the President came to Washington to become President of the United States, not to be my patient, and I think he feels that way. I think that he knows he does not have certain privileges when he is President. There are people who think that maybe it is OK for me and you to have our physicals every two, three, or four years, but he should have one every year. I don't know why he should have one every year if we only have ours every three or four years. I think it is difficult enough to see that he gets the care that ordinary citizens are accustomed to; that is hard enough.

MR. MEADOR: As I understand the description of your activities, you are with him almost constantly on out-of-town trips, and no one other than Mrs. Reagan perhaps is around him any more. What about day-to-day in the White House. Did you see him every single day?

DR. RUGE: I did not.

MR. MEADOR: Was there any pattern, every two or three days?

DR. RUGE: Well, he goes past the physician's office from the residence to the Oval Office. The doctor's office is where he gets off the elevator. He often sees me for what he called his sneeze shots, and incidentally, the doctor in California has remained his allergist. I mixed this potion and gave it to him. I would know when he would be going to his office, and maybe once a week I would stand out there, and he would say, "Is it time?" and I would say, "Yes, it's time." Sometimes I would be there just to wave at him, and he would ask the same question, "Is it time?" I would say no, I just want to let people know that I examine you and I have and you are fine, and stuff like that. I made it a big point not to see him because I think it is very awkward to have a doctor standing around one all of the time.

MR. THOMPSON: Did you have a backup?

DR. RUGE: Yes. First of all, and this has sort of been touched on a little bit, a committee would have never picked me as the doctor. When I was asked to be the doctor, I told Royal Davis that there are a lot of bright newcomers who want to make a name for themselves, and he gave me all of the reasons why that would be the worst kind to have. I was asked, and after two days, I decided I would do it. I also knew that I had not practiced in five years. I knew that I had not been an internist. I knew there were an awful lot of things in medicine that I did not know, and I was very fond of a young fellow who I had known since he was five years old. His name is Eric Louie. He went to grade school with my daughter. He went to Harvard Medical School, Harvard College, and he went to Andover. He was everything—AOA, Phi Beta Kappa, the works—and on two summer vacations he worked for me in Chicago. So I knew this fellow very well, and my wife had a bright idea, which was why don't you contact Eric because you feel this inadequacy, and in half a minute I realized that was one of the smartest things I have ever heard. So I called him; he was by that time a cardiologist fellow at Billings Hospital in Chicago. I proposed it to him, and he seemed very interested. I also had the good fortune of knowing Don Custis, who had been surgeon general of the Navy, and he and I had some conversations about this. As a matter of fact, Don was one of the first people I told about being asked to take the job. He said, "Why don't you go over and see Bill Cox," who was then surgeon general of the Navy, "and tell him what you want?" I said, "You mean I can just go over there?" He said, "Yes, after I call him." So he called him and told him who I was and what I wanted to do and I would like to see him. So I went to see Admiral Cox. He couldn't have been nicer. He was a little bit set back when I suggested somebody who wasn't in the service. He said if that's

29

what you want we'll do it. He couldn't have been better. He just greased the whole thing, and in no time at all Eric was out there for his physical and all of the paperwork, and Admiral Cox was just terrific. So they made Eric Louis a lieutenant commander, and he had two jobs so to speak, one in Bethesda and one here.

MR. MEADOR: Why did he have to have a military connection at all?

DR. RUGE: Somebody had to pay a salary.

MR. MEADOR: You had no military connections, though?

DR. RUGE: That's correct. But I told you earlier about members of the special support service to the president, and they are all military. I was the exception, and I was detailed over there by the VA, which was very nice because it was the highest salary. Some of the people at the White House were annoyed because I had a higher salary than George Bush. I had the second highest salary.

MR. MEADOR: Well, there have been physicians to the president in recent times, the last decade or so, brought in strictly from private practice of private life and just appointed to that position without any military connection. It that true or not? How about Kennedy's physician?

DR. RUGE: That is 25 years ago. That was Janet Travell, and she was the first one in many years. I was the second one in many years. The present physician is also a civilian. My guess is that the job will almost always go to a military physician. I think the Reagans are a little different.

(Break for Lunch)

(NOTE FROM DR. CRISPELL: There is a gap here. We are talking about members of the staff not telling the medical unit about trips with adequate time, and so forth.)

DR. RUGE: It was the first time that anybody in the medical unit heard it, we're going to Bogota, Colombia. This trip had been planned for a long time, and Eric said you had better talk to Ruge about that, and so they did. I said, sure, that wouldn't be a problem. It's 9,000 feet above sea level, and you go in over the mountains at 2,000 feet, but we did it. He could have become air sick. I resented certain things like that, and as a matter of fact, the people who were responsible for keeping it a secret put themselves in danger. There were people who made the decision for the trip and knew about the trip and were the ones who in a week or so left for South America on the survey of the trip, and they were not adequately protected vaccination-wise. If we had not found out in time, we would not have had the President in shape.

MR. THOMPSON: We've stepped off planes in Bogota when we went there, including doctors, and I saw a doctor keel over because of altitude.

DR. RUGE: I was really worried about that one. Then you get all kinds of suggestions such as maybe he should breathe loads and loads of oxygen before he gets off the helicopter. All that does is depress the respiratory system. We got even more suggestions after the first debate. That is when we got the suggestions such as pantyhose, hyperbaric chamber, the same drugs that Mondale was taking because apparently somebody thought it would lessen the nervous tension and he would perform better.

MR. MEADOR: You mean people were volunteering medical suggestions to you? Were these medical doctors?

DR. RUGE: Yes and no.

MR. THOMPSON: Is it your judgment that the personal physician serves a public purpose or a private purpose?

DR. RUGE: I think both. I think his primary purpose is to see to it that the President gets appropriate medical care, and I think that he knows that the assets of this country are there and he can ask

31

for anything that he wants, and he will get it. No one ever refuses the physician of the president anything. But I think the answer to "Are you serving the public?" is yes, you are. It is up to you to keep him as healthy as you can, and there you are serving the public too. I think the physician's opinions about some decision should be given some weight.

MR. THOMPSON: Could you have told the President, "Mr. President, I feel as your physician you're traveling too much"?

DR. RUGE: I would have if I felt that way. He really didn't travel that much. The other thing, Air Force I is pressurized differently than commercial airlines. He never has to carry anything he does not want to carry. I think that everyone else lives according to the President's schedule, and the President does not live according to anybody else's schedule very often. Everything is planned with his welfare in mind, in spite of the fact that there should be times when the physician ought to be involved in some of the decisions before they get as final as they are.

MR. THOMPSON: In retrospect, what do you think are the pros and cons of having a military officer as physician to the president?

DR. RUGE: Almost anytime I would have said it's perfectly OK. It probably is, and my guess is that is the way it's going to be. I was glad that I was not a military physician. I think it would be harder to be a president's physician in the military than not in the military. I think that Ed Cattau and I had quite a few conversations this last summer about that very thing. He would not like to be the President's physician.

MR. MEADOR: Could you explain a little bit more about why you say you would not want to be in the military and be the president's physician? What is the problem about that?

DR. RUGE: I think it could ruin your career. Even if you just appear to goof, it will ruin your career. I don't think military physicians' lives enable them to know as much about all of medicine as nonmilitary people know. I think by the time I became the President's physician I knew several good doctors in every city that we would be going to. I consider that a great advantage. I don't think that most military physicians have that kind of exposure or access in any of our usual lives. I think last summer when Nancy did not like what they were saying about her husband's cancer, they put a lid on the military physicians. I don't think anybody would have put a lid on me.

MR. MEADOR: Just because the military command of authority is present, it puts the physician in a different position. Is that what you mean? But he also has more media experience, I guess.

MR. THOMPSON: We saw the Arthur Miller program on presidents and illness on public television. Fred Friendly had organized the broadcast, and he had largely White House staff, Lloyd Cutler, a few senators, Ed Muskie, and some others. You went away feeling that there were a group of people who felt that they worked very closely with the President, they saw him under pressure, they knew what he could and could not do, and they were very impatient with the idea that any outside group, including the medical group, could judge him and his ability to serve any better than they could. So we have tentatively come to the conclusion that maybe it is this relation of the White House staff that's the single most crucial obstacle to any kind of medical role.

DR. RUGE: I think that is true. They have a proprietary attitude. It is their view that they know as much about him as any other group.

DR. DUVAL: I think you are investing it with more conscience than they deserve. I think your conclusion is correct. I'm not sure I would go with the process. I don't think it is exclusionary. I don't think these people think that way. If you have ever worked in that environment, these people eat, sleep, and drink what is on the agenda right now and what its ultimate political significance is. You can't do this, you can do this, you've got to do this, you've got to touch base. They don't think medically, and they don't think in terms of the President's confidence so that the result may be the same, but I don't think it is the fact, let's keep this to ourselves. I don't think that it is a consciously derived conclusion.

MR. THOMPSON: It is the work, then.

DR. RUGE: The nature of the work is absolutely preoccupying. I have never seen an environment like it.

MR. THOMPSON: Is it also survival of the state?

DR. RUGE: Absolutely, that maybe what drives them and the proximity of power. The election of 1984 meant more to them than it did to him.

DR. DUVAL: I would be interested, though, in extending the question you just asked, and Dan is in a good position to do it with respect to this President. We might all speculate with respect to any president. If it were left to the president at the beginning of, let's say, his or her elected term to identify that person to whom he hoped people would turn to make a judgment about his competence, what would be his response?

DR. RUGE: It's interesting you mentioned that because I wrote down here yesterday, what about the idea of having legislation that requires the president to designate a panel of three trusted, distinguished people, one of whom should be a physician, to make these kinds of judgments and then report to the vice president and the Congress.

DR. DUVAL: That is a potential solution. I was posing the question in the case specifically of Ronald Reagan. What is your beset judgment, to the extent you are willing to share it, as to whom he would suggest you turn to make a judgment about his competence if you wanted to check on it?

DR. RUGE: I think that he would have suggested his physician.

DR. DUVAL: You do, as opposed to Nancy?

DR. RUGE: Oh, yes. I think so.

DR. DUVAL: Would it be your perception, and anyone else for that matter, that this would be the inherently normal response of any person being elected president who is allowed to pick his own physician?

DR. RUGE: I was just going to add that. I think it is important that he be permitted to pick his physician. This idea of a committee doing an examination of the president and presidential candidates and then selecting the physician I think is wrong. I hate to be corny; I think it's un-American. I think in this country we have a right to make decisions even if they are wrong. That decision should not be taken from him.

DR. DUVAL: What would we do if the president selected a chiropractor?

DR. RUGE: Bush's physician was an osteopath who had an entirely different conception about how medicine should be practiced than what I had. As you know, there were some criticisms about selecting a neurosurgeon as the President's physician, and I thought it was answered very well, at least I liked the answer, by an internist who I knew when I was in the Navy. When I was in the Navy I was a board-certified neurosurgeon, but I did orthopedics, and we had a very fine young internist who was on the orthopedic service with me. When criticisms were raised, he wrote a letter to AMA News saying that he knew me in 1955 and I knew how to make referrals then and presumed that I still knew how to refer. He defended it. I also think that in being a neurosurgeon, a general surgeon, or a thoracic surgeon or something similar, one can have some advantages in the first place. Most of us don't have ego problems. I never felt emasculated by asking a specialist to take care of the President. As a matter of fact, I always insisted. I think that depending on the personality, a younger physician who was entirely family practice-oriented might feel a little bit of reluctance about referring a patient to a specialist. I have always noticed that super specialists are more inclined to refer than nonsuper specialists. What I originally said when asked was that I'm the wrong guy. Get yourself a bright internist; that's what you need. Loyal Davis said that was exactly what we don't want. We want a surgeon and we want a man who is old and I knew he had made up his mind. So that's why I took the job. I think that age and the fact that this really wasn't going to influence my career were assets to me.

DR. DUVAL: Could you have overridden the medical judgment of people that did care for the President?

DR. RUGE: I could have.

DR. DUVAL: You were a sort of gatekeeper.

DR. RUGE: Yes, but on the other hand, what I really did—and I think I did it right—was seek the help of the best people I could possibly get. This is one of the things that people really don't know; it all has to do with privacy. I had quite a few doctors see Ronald Reagan.
    Ronald Reagan was seen by one of the best-known opthalmologists in this town. He had doctors before he became president. We kept all of those people involved. I always talked to them. As a matter of fact, the internist about six months before I left thanked me for having kept him informed about these things. He said it was very nice to do that and that there was really no need for it. I think that I had probably the world's most famous hand surgeons see him. The people at Bethesda were all first class. I think that he was seen by a fair number of doctors in my four years.

DR. SCHWARZ: Let's assume a hypothetical case. You are concerned about his welfare, you've seen him in the hallway, maybe you see him more intensely. There's something big happening. The rest of the staff who are closest to him have done so too. Would you as physician to the President have the power or authority to demand to see him?

36

Kenneth R. Crispell, M.D.

DR. RUGE: Yes, I can see him anytime I want to see him. He almost always called me directly. But you are close to a problem. Presidents are very accustomed to having things done for them, and in this particular administration there was number-one advance man or a number-one planner of scenarios and so forth—Mike Deaver. I almost always would talk to the President and say, "Well, you've got to have this done." He would say he had told Mike to get it on the schedule. I thought that was not the right way. That is the old game of letting someone know that your position really isn't that important—we'll have one of my assistants notify the physician about something. Finally, one gets to the point where one of my assistants will advise one of his assistants on what should be done. I'm not quite Christian enough to accept that, but I put up with it. No, I think there is a problem there.

DR. CRISPELL: My summary of the situation is that you were the President's physician, but no one asked you to be politically involved. Is that fair?

DR. RUGE: Yes.

DR. CRISPELL: Unlike in the history of other physicians who have been very politically involved. Roosevelt's physician, Wilson's physician, and Janet Travell were much involved in writing silly statements as she did about Kennedy. You were not politically involved. Then you came to the point of crisis. On both occasions, the White House staff made decisions. There was no consultation. The final blow was when during the shooting episode, Fielding had the letter all ready for the President to sign.

MR. MEADOR: Was it a letter for the President to sign or a letter for the Cabinet and vice president to make the decision? I'm not clear on that.

DR. CRISPELL: Well, who knows the facts. We will have to ask Fred Fielding when he comes down. The interpretation is that Fielding had it ready, and there literally were two White Houses at that time. One was over at George Washington University, and one

37

was in the White House. In the White House when that letter came, Baker's assistant said, "I'll take it."

DR. RUGE: I know that because you have said so.

DR. CRISPELL: If Lawrence Barrett is correct, and he is a pretty honest reporter and spent a lot of time writing his book, when he was on the tape he again brought up the point that the President could have a letter ready, but the White House staff would not let him sign it. Where do we go from there in our thinking? Is there any way we can come up with a medical system to define inability? And even if we come up with that statement, where can we go from here?

DR. DUVAL: There ought to be a conversation as to whether or not this is in fact a medical problem. We may have our biases because we represent a certain background, and we may feel very keenly that this is something to be judged medically or at least there should be some substantially meaningful medical input. But I don't think it gives us the right to be arrogant. I think the issue ultimately is, what do you do in the case of the definition of inability to serve? That is a larger question in many people's minds than just medical. I would personally welcome some comment on it. If you are going to think over time and not under pressure of the recent assassination, to re-address the whole question of the Twenty-fifth Amendment, what are all of the elements that you would like to have brought into it to do it correctly and deliberately without being responsive to an immediate incident?

DR. CRISPELL: I agree with what you say. I think as doctors we like to muck around in power politics. But I think that the elected officials or their major appointed officials know more about the politics that are important to government than we do, although we may not think so at times. I think it is far better to have elected or major appointed officials making these decisions with the appropriate way for them to get the best medical advice.

38

DR. SCHWARZ: Do you think there is anything we would call "inability to serve" as physicians that any competent, intelligent person living with the President would not recognize?

MR. THOMPSON: Let me give one example, and then you can say whether this medically has any substance. What if someone, as it was said Mondale did, was on particularly strong antiblood pressure medicine? And what if I listened to him and thought, he's a little slower in his reactions than I remembered him 20 years ago, but on the other hand he has never been an orator. He has never done this or that. Wouldn't there be a difference between what you could ascertain? Isn't that an example of where you would know what effect it had on someone?

DR. RUGE: Yes, but it is not knowing what the effect is, but knowing whether there is enough wrong to impair the individual. I have asked this question not because I know the answer, but I have a feeling that we may tend to overdo it in terms of feeling that a physician has to initiate some kind of action if the President is impaired.

MR. MEADOR: As I understand what Ken Thompson is saying, medicine may have an effect on judgment, maybe on mental operations of a sort that a nonmedical person would not necessarily recognize. The medical person might know, given the facts about the medicine, that judgment is impaired. That seems to me a very plausible situation.

DR. RUGE: I think that the physician would recognize that someone was getting a little too hyper or a little agitated perhaps before someone else might or a little depressed.

DR. CRISPELL: In Mr. Mondale's case I have had enough experience with propanalol, and I am sure Tom has, that I do not want someone on propanalol deciding who is in charge of the football. I think I as a physician could tell when he was on it; I could also tell when this guy in Minnesota took him off of it.

DR. DUVAL: I think there is always an inherent wisdom to being ambiguous in extremely tough situations. I do not think there is any way one can anticipate everything, and I think it is a mistake generally to try to do something. So to me, there is a beauty in ambiguity. The thing that strikes me is the form of Sections 2, 3, and 4. No one has a problem with words that leave it totally to the President. The only exception is in Section 4 when someone from the outside says, I'm worried about this guy. That gives me a line of reasoning which suggests that all of these decisions should begin with the President or someone that close to him as possible, which is why I asked two questions of Dan. One, does he construe that the physician serves a public or a private purpose? I think that is a question that still could be discussed at considerable length because it goes beyond the question of confidentiality of a traditional physician-patient relationship. What we are talking about is, do you override the president in certain things if necessary to do so? So there is the issue of public purpose, and there is a second question. If it were going to be left to the president to make the determination and there was a concern about whether he could do so, who would he in his right mind have trusted to do so? And I think that is not an unimportant consideration. It might have been Nancy, and in this case it was Dan, and that is fine. Those are the avenues that I would probably pursue, but they do not necessarily limit themselves to medical applications.

MR. MEADOR: Well, you have an ultimate problem. Is there any way you can suggest having a more formalized institutionalized process that would ensure the integration of the medical judgments into the policy-making decision ultimately?

DR. DUVAL: Yes.

MR. MEADOR: What would be your suggestion beyond what we already have right there now?

DR. DUVAL: Probably his modification of the so-called Nebraska suggestion, which I think is the best think I have read of what Ken circulated.

MR. MEADOR: Did they give you a job description?

DR. RUGE: No.

MR. MEADOR: Is there one written?

DR. RUGE: I don't think so.

MR. MEADOR: It seems that one should be started so people would know what the responsibilities of the White House physician are.

DR. RUGE: I guess there is a job description for military people because we write them and do fitness reports.

DR. CRISPELL: Did you get clearance? Were you investigated by the FBI?

DR. RUGE: Yes.

DR. DUVAL: Let me ask a hypothetical question. The President was shot, was under lengthy surgery, and spent a long time under anesthesia. He came out of it, but you have a strange feeling that something is not right. That concern continues to grow. It may be early Alzheimer's, and it seems to accelerate. You are getting to the point where you are concerned about his ability to make judgments, and you believe that the other people around him are concerned. Would you have felt comfortable being the one to start the process and/or make the judgment about the degree in which he is impaired? Where do we get that judgment? We are all somewhat impaired. Under certain conditions, we are more impaired than others and there are certain judgments we have not business. I am talking about a president, let's say it is Reagan, and this happened and you are sitting there. What I think I am asking is, how do you start that process, and are you the right one to start it?

DR. RUGE: I don't know if I am the right one to start it, but I think that what I would do would be as I have said earlier, I would talk to him about it first and tell him my concern, and I would not let him or his wife talk me out of it.

MR. MEADOR: For example, could you imagine under certain circumstances going to the vice president to say, "I believe that the President is really not up to it, and it seems to me there ought to be a vote by you and the Cabinet"?

DR. RUGE: I had a feeling that I knew William French Smith well enough to have a conversation with him. I found out as much as I could about William French Smith, and maybe I was naive at some point, but I looked upon him as the lawyer of the administration and not Fred Fielding. I would have found a way of talking to him. I would not have gone through the West Wing. I made up my mind about that very early, and it was not that I disliked them because I did not dislike them. But I thought of both George Bush and the attorney general, and those are the two I would have talked to.

DR. KNORR: It seems as though all of the conditions that are being mentioned are mental. Even with the lung wound he was not incapable because he had a bullet in the lung. He was incapable because anesthesia depressed him mental processes. I cannot think of any physical condition that would make one incapable of functioning. It has to be the mental result of the physical condition. That can be very subtle, as in the case you mentioned. In early Alzheimer's it is difficult for people to say, for instance, that Uncle Joe is getting a little funny, and when you try to discover what that comment is about, you never quite discuss it.

MR. MEADOR: Suppose there was a case in which the president was in a serious accident and was a total paraplegic with no use of any muscles, totally bedridden, could not feed himself, lost control of bowel movements, and so forth, but not impairment of the mind. Would your point hold that this is not the kind of inability we contend with?

DR. RUGE: I would think so, and I think those people interested in the rehab movement today would be very angry with him for using that example that someone who is paraplegic is disabled. They would say that he is disabled but not handicapped.

MR. MEADOR: So it will be a minor problem no matter how serious the physical impairment is.

DR. KNORR; It is the mental impairment associated with the physical problem that would make him incapable. It was back in the early 1950s, I think 1951 at Bethesda, but this is not really known. I have never seen it written, but Alban Barkley is vice president, and he came into Bethesda Hospital. I guess he was about 73 years of age. It was noticed in the evenings that he was sundowned, meaning that he was a little disoriented and didn't know where he was. You take some elderly people out of their usual environment and this can happen. The nursing staff was quite concerned. Be sure that you keep an eye on the vice president, that sort of thing. I wonder if something had happened to Truman how capable was the vice president. This conversation we are having should perhaps be extended to, if the president is incapable, is the vice president really capable? In 1952 he suggested or indicated that he was going to run, but he was not the candidate Adlai Stevenson chose as vice president. In 1954 he ran for Senate again and was elected and then died just a few months after that at age 79. I wonder if the Senate committee that was mentioned had Alban Barkley in mind when they talked about those hearings? That could have been very difficult. He was fine all day and in the evening did not quite know where he was, what time it was, could not get his wits about him, and then the next morning was up and about fine again.

MR. THOMPSON: What if you had the opposite? The most plausible explanation I've heard was what Rusk said last week about LBJ. There are all kinds of theories, but he said that LBJ felt he was living on borrowed time and that is why he had this impulse to get up at three in the morning and continue to keep driving. He thought he did not have time, and what if someone is impulsively driving himself that way. Isn't that kind of quicksand if one were to try to judge that?

DR. KNORR: Suppose you had someone like the character in the Caine Mutiny whose behavior is just a little bit different. Would you have felt that he was incapable of leadership? The trial, of course, was a difficult thing when these people took over the ship because they really could not prove that, and the man finally did himself in.

MR. MEADOR: This seems kind of nitpicky, but on my extreme total paraplegic case where there is no impairment of mind but everything else is gone, one of the duties of the president is to sign bills enacted by Congress. They don't become law without his signature. He is unable to sign bills, yet that is one of his duties. What do you think about that? Is that not the kind of thing we are concerned with, though?

DR. RUGE: We have a president who has a physical problem to write. I think he could probably get around that.

DR. SCHWARZ: They could figure out through the computer, and he could sign a name. The communication's media has overcome much of that disability in actual signing.

DR. KNORR: In a hypothetical instance, are you talking about an individual who is elected by the American people after he was quadriplegic?

MR. MEADOR: I had not thought about a particular distinction.

DR. KNORR: But the distinction I think has merit if for no other reason then that if that was the choice of the American people, you would say it was their mandate.

MR. MEADOR: Politically speaking, I think there is a world of difference if someone is elected in the state he is in. Politically, it would be inconceivable that anyone would consider removing him. On the other hand, . . .

DR. CRISPELL: Would you enlarge on your point that this is not medical?

DR. KNORR: I don't think I said that. I said it isn't exclusively medical.

DR. CRISPELL: What did you say, then?

DR. KNORR: Ken Thompson put it better. The issue is, how do you intelligently integrate an appropriately derived medical judgment that was not wholly dependent on only one person into a collective political judgment? I think that is the bottom-line question that you are talking about with respect to Section 4. I think that medical judgment cannot prevail, but there has to be intelligent medical judgment that comes into the process and then it must in turn be integrated. Here is where you would get into the question, do you involve Congress? Do you involve the Supreme Court? Should it be within the Cabinet? Is the separation of powers involved? All of the questions that the lawyers are good at. I am not discounting medical, but I am not giving it the exclusive right to make a judgment.

DR. CRISPELL: Let me go theoretical one more time. I guess I am not disturbed by what Monty says; I am encouraged that maybe we are getting there. Dan, one year from now President Reagan says he has a headache, and obviously the first thing you are going to do is a CAT scan of his brain. He has already got a cancer, or MRI, one or the other; he has a metastasis, and that's very possible. Who would you call on? Is that medical?

DR. RUGE: Sure.

DR. CRISPELL: Damn right it's medical. You don't want someone with a metastatic brain lesion deciding about the football. I don't care where the lesion is because all you picked up on the MRI is the big one. He hasn't really shown any change in personality except that he has a headache. This is where I think the vice president has to have someone to go to and say, this is a serious medical problem that will eventually impair his judgment.

DR. RUGE: You mean the physician has to have someone to go to?

DR. CRISPELL: Well, the vice president initiates all of this.

DR. RUGE: Yes, but I mean how will he know about the headache?

DR. CRISPELL: I didn't say it in the right order. He has to go to the vice president and say here's the problem, now where do we go from there?

DR. DUVAL: The Nebraska solution very intelligently in my judgment leaves the vice president out of the room in toto. He is never involved. He avoids the catch-22 situation you have described so well. What happens is that the physician in this instance would invoke the selection of three physicians that are chosen by the secretary of the treasury or what have you. They make a medical judgment, that judgment is reported to the Cabinet, the Cabinet makes a decision and then informs the vice president. Now, I am not saying it is a perfect solution. But I would submit that this has been a well-thought-out type of approach that does attack some of the problems you have asked us to consider and maybe needs improving upon. It does have the desirable feature that it is number one on the executive side; second, it leaves out the party most at interest, which is the vice president, until the decision is made; and third, it involves important, in fact primary, medical input without it prevailing. That is to me the beauty of the Nebraska approach.

MR. MEADOR: Dan would approach that by going directly to the president and saying, you've got a lesion in your head.

DR. DUVAL: Suppose he said, "Ain't nothing wrong with me, Dan; I'm doing fine."

DR. CRISPELL: Well, Dan would go ahead.

DR. RUGE: It is very difficult to hide a president. The things like those involving Woodrow Wilson, Franklin Roosevelt, and JFK would be impossible to pull off today. Presidents have their pictures in the papers all the time, and they're missed. Roosevelt was out of the country for weeks at a time and we didn't even know about it. I must say I have always been rather jealous of the way Cleveland's doctors handled it. I would have been very proud to have been a part of that company. I bet it was a lot of fun.

DR. CONNALLY: Lyndon Johnson had a coronary. I don't think anyone knows about it, not the one in Charlottesville. This was one at the time of Churchill's funeral. They sent Earl Warren as our official representative. Everyone was wondering why the vice president didn't go. Johnson did not have a cold; he had a coronary.

DR. CRISPELL: The first one?

DR. CONNALLY: It wasn't the first one. His first one was around 55. This one he had when he was president, but no one knew about it.

MR. MEADOR: You mean vice president, or president?

DR. CONNALLY: President. This was when Humphrey stayed in the country and Earl Warren went to Churchill's funeral not because he had a bad cold but because Johnson had had a coronary.

DR. DUVAL: If the president's physician is going to be involved, I think that the job description of his responsibility to the public as well as to the president needs to be set forth. I think Dan has the good fortune of being the physician to a president with unusual

47

physical attributes. I don't think of any president in the past that I can remember that even comes close.

MR. MEADOR: Let me ask Dr. Ruge this question. When you were first appointed and took office, did you have any conversation at all of any substance with the outgoing physician of the president; that is, President Carter.

DR. RUGE: Yes, I did, and Dr. Lukash was wonderful.

MR. MEADOR: One conversation or several?

DR. RUGE: One very good one and one very short one. The nice thing about him was that I think he was ready to quit. He had been there for 14 years. He physicianed two presidents, and the best thing he did for me was—I only worked a block away from the White House—that he saw to it that I could come over and visit with his entire staff. We had only one real heart-to-heart talk about this, and that is the conversation in which he said that the important thing is to take care of the president, and all you have to do as far as the public is concerned is to tell them if he is well or if he isn't well. I think we had very frank discussions. He told me various things that he had been thinking about in the last eight years.

MR. MEADOR: When did you first become aware of the Twenty-fifth Amendment?

DR. RUGE: I have always had a little bit more than the usual interest in current events.

MR. MEADOR: So it wasn't at the time you became the physician?

DR. RUGE: No.

DR. CRISPELL: Did Dr. Lukash tell you that they had had the papers all ready for Carter's hemorrhoid surgery?

DR. RUGE: No, he didn't mention it. We didn't discuss it.

Kenneth R. Crispell, M.D.

DR. CRISPELL: Has the new man asked you anything?

DR. RUGE: He and I probably had more conversations than any other two physicians. The new man and I have known each other for almost five years now, and he was at the White House three or four times during my time. When the President had a urological problem, I called him. I had his former physician, who is the new man come in, and we put him up in a hotel in Georgetown and he went to Bethesda where the President had his urological evaluation. He was a urologist; he is the one who did the TUR about 25 years ago, and we sort of kept him a secret, but after everything turned out OK, I asked Deaver if we could have him rid back to the White House in a helicopter, so everyone saw this doctor off with the President. We did not announce that he was going to be here. There is no point in having the whole country worked up to a frenzy by the press. We had many discussions. We has almost all of them before he arrived.

MR. THOMPSON: Would you agree that one part of this problem of the physician telling the president that he is unable to serve is the finality of it all? Churchill stepped down from power but then he came back, and then he was out again. I did a book on Churchill, so I read all of the speeches. He continued to make speeches, and he continued to be an influential political figure. We cut former presidents off; we don't do it with academic people. If you can't handle a big class anymore, you take a smaller class or you go into research or you do something else. We don't make use of our former presidents except for funerals. It's little wonder that Wilson or any president would resist leaving the office. I would wonder if he wouldn't be somewhat inhibited to step down.

DR. RUGE: He enjoys being president. It's a great job and you meet a lot of nice people, and he thinks he will leave his mark on the country. I don't think it makes a heck of a lot of difference to him whether he is president or isn't.

MR. THOMPSON: More to Nancy or less?

DR. RUGE: I think more to her than to him and I think that when the children say he would never have been president without her that there is an element of truth to it. He also had an awful lot of friends who wanted him to be president, and it was his friends who made him governor of California. People such as Holmes Tuttle and Justin Dart raised the money in one afternoon for the first campaign as governor. I think he became president so darn easily that it really didn't matter. He would have liked to have been president sooner, we all know that. But I'll bet he did not feel down for more than about one day after he was defeated by Ford for nomination in 1976.

MR. THOMPSON: An ambitious president's wife would have a lot of bearing on what happened if you went to tell him he was not able to serve.

DR. SCHWARZ: Do you think if he had Alzheimer's and was having some memory impairment that he could utilize Section 3 without your having to impose Section 4?

DR. RUGE: I think there would be a problem because I'm pretty sure that anyone who has Alzheimer's disease probably would have difficulty knowing that he ought to invoke the Twenty-fifth Amendment. Isn't that true?

DR. KNORR: There is a time when they feel they are slipping and they can't quite explain why. It's very early on.

DR. RUGE: I think it would be a problem even with him. I think there would be a problem. And I don't think you could talk him out of the White House in a day.

MR. MEADOR: Aren't there two kinds of inability? One is a permanent one, which Alzheimer's would be; it's not going to get any better. The other would be the temporary one. For example, the heavy drinking problem. If the president develops a bad enough drinking problem so that every day from about 6:00 p.m. on he was really out of it, I could suppose you could make a pretty fair argument to him and invoke Section 3 until he got himself straightened out. Either take a cure or whatever for two, three, or four months—whatever it took—and regain his powers. That's the surgery think we had last summer. Short run, temporary, maybe not so short run, but temporary. The other is forever giving up, and that is Ken Thompson's point. He's not going to want to do that.

MR. THOMPSON: From the standpoint of doctors, would you agree with Bill Rogers (former secretary of state) that as you view it, the Twenty-fifth Amendment is probably as good a piece of legislation as we have? Herbert Brownell had a hand, along with Birch Bayh. And Bill Rogers would be glad to say I'll be glad to talk with you, glad to see anyone, but I don't think you are going to improve the Twenty-fifth Amendment. I just wonder what reaction you have to that?

DR. RUGE: I tend to agree with that. I am not at all comfortable going very far in my own mind trying to define more clearly what constitutes inability to serve. I would be much more comfortable setting up a mechanism for people to judge on an individual case.

MR. MEADOR: The vice president has veto power over the whole thing according to the Twenty-fifth Amendment. He has to, along with the Cabinet officers, but they cannot do it alone without his having initiated it.

DR. CRISPELL: You don't need an initiator as a vice president?

MR. MEADOR: He may not be the initiator, but he must concur in the judgment.

DR. CRISPELL: He's got veto power.

MR. MEADOR: Now there can be another group other than the Cabinet. Congress may prescribe another group, but the vice president still will have to join in the decision.

DR. DUVAL: I have two concerns about Section 4. One is the fact that I'm discomforted, and I think I expressed this earlier, by having the most important person who is going to be the presumed beneficiary also a part of the solution. The second thing that I am anxious about is that it is possibly unnecessarily cumbersome and unwieldy. It could take a long time for them to go into all of the various ramifications depending upon the circumstances. It could take a month. So those are my two reservations about Section 4. I don't really have any difficulty with the first three sections of Twenty-fifth Amendment.

MR. STEPHAN: The one thing that cannot be modified under Section 4 is the vice president's consent. He has to be accountable for the initiation.

DR. DUVAL: That would require another amendment?

DR. CRISPELL: That would mean rewriting Section 4.

MR. MEADOR: I was assuming that you could do a lot of other things by legislation and that would not need an amendment.

MR. STEPHAN: One of the things that you are trying to relieve is the discomfort on the part of the vice president. The tremendous ambivalence that he would feel is that the whole thing would go through a process before he gave his imprimatur right at the end. Yet that would relieve him of some of the ambivalence or discomfort.

MR. MEADOR: You are suggesting that Congress could prescribe a procedure through which this decision is to be made that would bring the vice president in at a later point following initiatives by another group before he became involved?

MR. STEPHAN: Only at the end.

MR. MEADOR: Well, it seems to me that might well be done.

MR. STEPHAN: Only at the end, and what I am trying to do is avoid another amendment to the Constitution.

DR. CRISPELL: I think you could find a group of physicians, but he would have to get them to the task by evaluating the president in a very short period of time because with time they would tend to develop the same kind of denial mechanisms that the president and his Cabinet and everyone else associated with the president could develop regarding his inability to serve.

MR. MEADOR: You could create a new three-doctor panel every New Year's day. You need them in place, don't you, in case they have to be called on?

DR. DUVAL: You get them in place and they have time to figure out in their own head over time their feelings about the man, and you are going to get a much different evaluation than if you would just tell them and get it done very quickly. I may be wrong. I would be interested in what Dan thinks about that. Do you think that there is a chance that a doctor would join the denial that the president is incapable along with the other people surrounding the president? Is there a chance?

DR. RUGE: I think it would be very remote.

DR. CRISPELL: Do you think you could maintain your objectivity regarding the inability to serve?

DR. RUGE: I think so. I think I could.

MR. MEADOR: Well, if you could, maybe you could a panel too. I am concerned about the enormous responsibility. Did you ever think of that or worry about that?

DR. RUGE: Yes, I worried about it.

DR. DUVAL: One way to sharpen this would be to get either the Cabinet or some other appointed group who would serve the role as the Cabinet here to make the determination to pass on to the vice president and set up several ways in which they can get medical judgment from time to time and have consultation with the president's physician. If they feel this is inadequate, maybe at that time you could have some mechanism by which they could get another panel of physicians. I would think that the legislation should be pointed toward that group and then give them some leeway or suggestions as to how they should get medical judgment.

MR. THOMPSON: Is there any trend in the medical profession, leaving aside emotion and loyalty toward a president, of pushing physicians in the direction of not committee themselves strongly both institutionally and personally? I have seen personally that doctors do not take a stand in a great many institutional cases. They don't want to play God, and this in a way is playing God, isn't it?

DR. CRISPELL: Certainly. All you have to do is to get beat up in court a few times.

DR. SCHWARZ: It is like a faculty member making a tough judgment on whether a student ought to be dismissed or not, and after you go through the hearings, you have a hesitancy to do what is right. Back to a question I asked earlier and Monty refined it, to what extent do you feel as a physician to the president any conflict between your personal responsibility to him and the public responsibility to everyone else? Is that a major source of conflict? Should those two functions be separated?

DR. RUGE: It would certainly be easier if it were that way, there is no doubt about that. I'm glad it never became a problem. I thought about it being a problem many times, and I know very well that I could have had a hard time, but I would never have done anything without talking to him. There is another thing too, and that is a president so exposed that there is almost nothing that can be hid. I'm talking about today. There were a lot of implications tossed around after the first debate, if you remember.

MR. THOMPSON: Fatigue in Louisville.

DR. RUGE: Yes. I have often thought that there is more of a chance of a competent president being called incompetent than a incompetent president being called competent. Also, very early in the administration he had a cold, and he was having all of these senators go up to the residence. A lot of the press knew that he had a cold. People such as Helen Thomas were wondering, is he really well? It almost seemed to me that more people were calling him ill when he was not ill than would have been the case otherwise. But I doubt that you could have a Wilson or Roosevelt situation today. One of the things that would make it easy for a physician to assert himself or not quite as difficult is because this country is so health conscious.

MR. MEADOR: Someone earlier raised the question about having some sort of job description for the president's physician. Would there be any merit in at least recommending a code of conduct for the president's physician in which there would be some effort to articulate these responsibilities? Would there be any value in trying to set that out in writing established either by custom or in some other formal way that every physician felt legitimized it or formally sorted out these roles?

DR. RUGE: I think it would make it easier for the physician. It seems to me that it is a touchy business. If you start having some kind of code that spells out obligations to the public, it is very tempting on the part of some people to include in those obligations to tell them what his daily blood pressure is or to get it that detailed. Somehow it would have to be worked out so that it is an obligation that deals with the ability to serve.

DR. CRISPELL: One the thing comes to mind that I don't think has been discussed. There is no question that Roosevelt's physician, Wilson's physician, and Janet Travell became politicized.

DR. DUVAL: Suppose we said from now on we are going to write a law and here is what the law is going to say. First, every president is obligated to select the person who is going to be his personal physician. Second, a panel of three physicians irrespective of how they are put in place must also be appointed. We will talk about the procedure of how. Third, the fundamental purpose of the president's physician is to serve the president and he must do that first and must also keep the president wholly and totally informed of his own; that is, the physician's deliberations and thoughts. Fourth, any action that comes under Section 4 must invoke that panel of three physicians and it will be the body that joins with the vice president and the Cabinet that makes the final determination. Now what I'm attempting to suggest is that the medical profession has powerful input to give but should by no means make the decision. The vice president should not be involved as the final arbitrator. These decisions should never devolve upon single individuals. That's what I am suggesting. That is not leaving the medical profession out.

DR. CRISPELL: That's bringing it in in a different way.

DR. DUVAL: I suggest a way in which they cannot get there without that panel of three. It is an essential cog in the machine, but it could not make the final judgment. It can only react to the medical judgment that is brought to it. I might add that the group should by law be forced to meet four times a year to review everything known about the president's health so that there becomes an increasing body of knowledge that they share about the president even though they are not the president's personal physician.

MR. MEADOR: Do you have any ideas about how that threesome would be chosen?

DR. DUVAL: This is not a putdown, but I think that is easy. You could do the same thing the secret service does vis-à-vis treasury; you can turn to the department and have them put in three. You could have the Supreme Court pick one, someone from the Senate pick one, the physician could join the other two and pick the third. I can think of machinery. I am not greatly bothered by that. I'm more interested in the principle of getting away from the single person having too much power in a government that operates the way ours does.

DR. HOGNESS: What about the general confidentiality of the experience? Suppose the president were sleeping with his secretary and this by everyone who knew him improved his ability to govern and this group found out about it. I think there are some things the president might do that ought never to be known by anyone. I agree with that wholly and totally, but the presumption is that it hasn't made him unable, so to speak, to serve.

DR. DUVAL: Let's say that this is a symptom that the process driving the behavior is something much more insidious and has much more insidious implications for his ability to serve than it did in that instance.

DR. CONNALLY: You are speaking of alcoholism?

MR. THOMPSON: What would be the best mechanism, Dr. Duval, for further study and for the putting forward of the idea with some expectation that people would take it clearly? Would it be a series of studies? Would it be a book by you? Would it be a commission? What would it be?

DR. DUVAL: I don't have any idea. I would suppose that the way to get attention would be to have incidences reviewed of the presidency such as Roosevelt. Perhaps one of the large private foundations could endorse or underwrite a study that would culminate in a Carnegie Commission Report on the presidency or some such. It should derive from some relatively neutral and impartial point of origin as opposed to someone who has a stake in the process. Look at this as an intellectual question as we bring the 20th century to a close. I have not thought about this problem at all really until today.

MR. MEADOR: Suppose we were going to have a commission of 15 or 18 persons or whatever. I wonder if you or anyone else around the table has suggestions of the types of persons you would pull together to constitute such a commission?

DR. DUVAL: You are speaking of this line Section 4 or such other bodies . . .

MR. MEADOR: No. I'm talking about a commission to study the problem.

DR. DUVAL: If I thought, with all due respect to Roy, that it was being promulgated by the AMA, for instance, because medicine wanted a bigger hand in determining, I think this would be a tactical mistake.

MR. MEADOR: You would want some medical doctors on this commission?

DR. DUVAL: Yes, although I might quality that and say I don't think it would make any difference. I have a feeling ironically that the voice of medicine in the room could be even more powerful it if wasn't present. There are a lot of these judgments that will be made medically, and there are people in the room who are not themselves medical people who invoke the role of medicine. My suggestion would be that there be a thoughtful medical person in the room. I'm thinking out loud. I think we ought to try to avoid giving anyone the impression that this arises because someone has an interest in the medical result.

MR. MEADOR: Say you had a commission even though they could not really come up with much in the way of new legislation or any formal institution or apparatus they would want to install. It occurs to me there might be some value in publishing a report that simply spotlights the problem and in effect puts pressure on the White House staff and Cabinet to be alert to it. The process might improve it in the future a little bit and make people more conscious of it or alert to it.

DR. RUGE: It would enhance the awareness of the problem.

MR. MEADOR: I don't think you ought to stop there. If that is the only impact you have, it would still be worth doing. I think we ought to set our goals and sights on something much larger.

MR. STEPHAN: Does anyone have any problem with the Cabinet being the major group making this decision? Would it be better for Congress to pass some legislation that may be allowed by the amendment that would have another body which would actually make the decision?

DR. DUVAL: As to some things, as the Nebraska proposal. I think this might have been Eisenhower's thinking. The vice president ought to stand apart from the press. Nixon changed from originally favoring the outside approach to favoring the approach that was enacted. Private citizen Nixon in the 1960s. Feeling that the vice president was showing that it be held accountable to the decision whether or not he participated and it was believed that he would, he might as well be up front about it. It was his responsibility, and if something as momentous as unseating the president took place and the person who would bear the consequences, then the person who replaced him ought to go along with the decision.

MR. MEADOR: Wasn't there also some element there that, including vice president and Cabinet, you have the kind of intimate top-level executive family all of the same political party as the president rather than having any kind of extraneous outside elements?

COMMENT: That is not as clear as Dan, because there are plenty of precedents without outside elements. At the time that Truman succeeded Roosevelt, the secretary of state was a Republican, so Truman could have been succeeded at that time before the 1947 act by the secretary of state was next in line.

MR. STEPHAN: I think it is clear from looking at the record that at least the vocalized reservations were not that the process would not be effective enough, but that it might be too effective, that people were concerned about making it hard rather than easy. And indeed, if you look at it, it is harder to invoke Section 4 than it is to invoke the impeachment process. You can get a president impeached with a majority of the House. However, it takes two-thirds of both the House and the Senate to remove a disabled person if there is a dispute. So the part of the thinking of making it hard rather than easy was to make sure that the people who were most immediately involved had a voice. People who would be either elected or confirmed by the Senate as opposed to staff would be responsible.

MR. THOMPSON: It is a big issue on both succession and on this. Truman favored someone the people had elected. It is the American people speaking through the ballot box to the selection of an individual. That is what is being preserved through all of the process. The question of separation of powers is all very interesting, and I think for legal scholars it must be terribly important. To me it is not an issue; it stays within the executive branch with appropriate constraints. I have no difficulty in going back to what Dan has said. I have no difficulty personally with the four articles as they exist beyond what I said about the cumbersomeness of Section 4. But I am very much persuaded by the type of conversation we have had today that there may be utility in looking at a smaller step between 3 and 4, something that you have to go through by law to invoke Section 4. That is to say, something that the vice president has to do before the majority or whatever can actually take an action. That's where I would come down. We ought to focus on that unless you agree that we don't need any further treatment of this issue at all. Do you think that the public feels that we need further treatment on this? That the public is aware of the problem?

DR. DUVAL: No, but on the other hand, I was the general public yesterday, and I didn't feel the need to know.

DR. CRISPELL: Eleven times in the last three years I have talked to various groups—physicians, laymen, young people, old people—and I can assure you that only about 10 percent of the public even know what the Twenty-fifth Amendment is, including three of my associates on the law faculty that I tested.

DR. DUVAL: Well, if you had asked me before you called me up I wouldn't have known what the Twenty-fifth Amendment was.

MR. MEADOR: If lack of public awareness were the governing consideration, we wouldn't be giving attention to a whole lot of things which are important.

DR. DUVAL: Half of the people in the United States cannot name the vice president.

DR. CRISPELL: My concern is terrorism and the bomb. I think we have to know that the president is capable of communicating and making decisions.

MR. MEADOR: Isn't that element—that is, the intercontinental ballistic missile and the nuclear device—the one that gives all of this an urgency? We wouldn't be nearly as concerned about it, I expect, if it weren't for that element.

DR. CRISPELL: We have had people sick in all branches. I am sure you looked up Frankfurter's history when you had Douglas as a patient. Mrs. Frankfurter took him in and sat him up for 18 months. No one as far as we can find out, except that we know nothing about the national defense commission, but the president is the one that can put that thing in the computer, that little card. So it seems to me there is a real reason for setting up the mechanism, whether it is three doctors or what, and I am intrigued now with keeping the vice president out of it until some decision has been made otherwise. I think the senator will tell us that they try to avoid anything that would look like a coup. If you read the tone in the hearings, it is sort of in between the lines. We can't set up a situation that you have in South America.

DR. SCHWARZ: I think we've got to follow the first rule that we ought to follow in medicine. First, do no harm and you have to be careful that you are not setting up something that absolutely makes the odds greater of causing some squabble or coup or a period of ambivalence about who was the president or had presidential authority. The possibility of having that may be greater than the possibility of having the government out of action due to a disabled president.

DR. DUVAL: That is exactly why I am surprised that the vice president plays such a prominent role. He has to live with the consequences. Maybe he wants to. He is the most obvious person.

MR. THOMPSON: Is there any chance that if we got a good report and it stood up in the minds of those of you who are professional in this area that your groups might want to call it to the attention of someone? I wrote the report on the president and Congress in foreign policy for the Association of Former Members of Congress and the Atlantic Council. Ed Muskie and Ken Rush were co-chairmen, and a report was issued last May. There were a handful of reporters at the press conference, and Muskie and Rush met with congressional staffers and it dropped like a pebble to the bottom of the well. No one picked it up, and that is one thing we thought of with this initiative. If there were groups who spoke with some authority who at least would promote the further discussion of it in their circles, it might make more of a ripple.

DR. SCHWARZ: First of all, definitely there are. I would presume the AMA, for example. I agree that the AMA should not in any way initiate it from the beginning. Second, it is a very different copy in a time where the President has had a couple of problems that I think would almost be automatic to create attention.

MR. MEADOR: It is an interesting happenstance that with this president, there have been two situations that provide interesting case studies. It is just a happenstance that they are in this administration. But I don't view that as an argument militating against doing the study. It seems to me on the contrary that it gives you the happy circumstance of some specific cases.

DR. HOGNESS: How long do you think it would take to do such a study? A couple of years?

MR. THOMPSON: It has with other groups.

DR. HOGNESS: There is another argument. By that time, Ronald Reagan is going to be at the end of his term or pretty close to it. So in no way could it be interpreted as being directed at him except for a six-month period.

DR. CRISPELL: John, just suppose that he has two or three more press conferences that went like the Louisville debate—one right after another. Let's say he does show signs of fatigue. I think the focus would be pretty sharp on him. If we had a three to four member commission, could we name them by position?

DR. HOGNESS: With totally ex officio powers.

DR. CRISPELL: I mean automatic, undersecretary of health, head of the NIA. You would let the president do this? I am talking about the three MDs. The question is, should we have a panel of physicians, and if we name them instead of Joe Blow, it's the undersecretary for health, it's the director of the NIA, president of the National Academy of Medicine, and so forth.

MR. MEADOR: In many ways it has to be a physician by any statutory concern.

DR. CRISPELL: They have by tradition.

MR. MEADOR: What if you had the president pick them from a list of 12 provided by the AMA? Or the Bar Association?

DR. CRISPELL: Where do we stand with John Chancellor? Did he ever call back?

MR. THOMPSON: No.

DR. CRISPELL: Did anyone hear Chancellor saying that there had to be someone in between?

MR. THOMPSON: You have many scholars on presidential illness here. Does anyone think that the country would have been well served by the Twenty-fifth Amendment having been invoked for any president since Wilson?

DR. CRISPELL: Early in Roosevelt. Roosevelt was sicker than hell for 20 years. His blood pressure was 190 over 100 in 1932 when he was governor of New York.

MR. MEADOR: I don't understand your answer to his question. What are you saying about Roosevelt?

DR. CRISPELL: I don't think you could have invoked the amendment. Who else would have taken over? But I'm saying if there was someone who says that hypertensive disease that could not be treated and they said that in 1936, I think it would have.

MR. THOMPSON: I think historians would say he ranks right up there with Washington, Lincoln, and Jefferson.

DR. CRISPELL: Historians have absolutely no interest in illness, I can tell you. I have talked to the star of stars at our place, and he said it does not make a difference.

DR. HOGNESS: What about the panel being made up of the president of the American College of Physicians, the president of the American College of Surgeons, and one other person? They change every year; therefore, you don't have this idea of them thinking . . .

DR. CRISPELL: What I would like is something that names not by position.

DR. HOGNESS: An ex officio commission.

Kenneth R. Crispell, M.D.

DR. CRISPELL: Of eminence. Yes, and I have not difficulty with that. As I said, to me that is a process that you could go over a day or two with a group of intelligent people.

MR. MEADOR: I think that is a very good point. Of course, it is fundamental, but don't underestimate the difficulty of deciding how those three are to be chosen. That is the kind of thing you get hung up on politically and for an indefinite length of time. People are going to view that as really a very sensitive and touchy situation; who are those three going to be? I don't think that is an insignificant little side point that can be sorted out in a half hour's discussion.

DR. DUVAL: We could start off by saying, well, it could be the four surgeons dinner. There is another one that says as I said that I threw something loose out of the other the day. We could have one that is appointed by the president that is the president's physician, and he joins with the Speaker of the House and picks the second and then with the president pro tem of the Senate they pick the third. Or give the president a slate of a dozen and tell him to pick three. I can think of ways. I would like to hear some discussion about the merits of each of those types. But we do the selection process all of the time every state goes through it, picking a state licensing board. We go through it with all sorts of things. We have many precedents is what I am saying. It is much easier for me to deal with that subject in my mind than it is the principles that I think are very profound that you are touching upon.

DR. CRISPELL: I don't think you answered the question that Tom asked relative to anyone thinking the Twenty-fifth Amendment should have been invoked on the president since Wilson. I think he was asking, if it had been invoked would there be a different course of history, and to that I would say yes.

DR. CONNALLY: The people who come to mind, I guess, are Franklin Roosevelt's hypertension at the end of his term, maybe Lyndon Johnson hit the bottle too hard, Nixon's drug and alcohol problem at the end of his term, and Eisenhower, with a couple of strokes. I don't know if we would improve things by any of the proposed mechanisms.

MR. MEADOR: In the first place, look at Franklin Roosevelt. It gets back up to the point that someone raised earlier today. He was elected by the people to a fourth term; he lived only three or four months. Do you think immediately following the election that anyone would have considered invoking the Twenty-fifth Amendment?

DR. DUVAL: A judgment of this kind should be left to the elective process because the people are not able to understand the data or come to a conclusion based on it.

MR. MEADOR: I think if you had the Twenty-fifth Amendment, Eisenhower might easily have invoked a section of it himself for a little while. He had this letter of understanding, you know, with Nixon on which the Twenty-fifth Amendment was designed in a sense to formalize that process and replace that old informal letter of understanding.

DR. CRISPELL: Section 3 is almost a verbatim copy of the Eisenhower letter.

MR. THOMPSON: Is there any merit to thinking of two different circumstances under which and mechanisms under which some action could be invoked? One, a national emergency, and two, all other situations. I do not know who declares a national emergency, but could you have a special emergency mechanism if you had a nuclear attack?

DR. CRISPELL: A fast mechanism. The one that has been suggested is that the chief justice pro tem and the House could say, "Bang, there's an emergency."

DR. DUVAL: Let's assume that we recommend, those of us who are here with or without the folks from Virginia, that we ought to go another step that some national commission ought to be established—a committee to look at this in depth and analyze it and to make recommendations because we are very concerned about the process. How do we see us going to that stage and under whose auspices and how do we move that into a action that I would gather there is a consensus for?

MR. THOMPSON: The way we have done it with the other groups is that we have tried to get a sense of who we thought were the people most directly involved whom authorities thought would provide the best leadership for it. And then, although we make suggestions to the people who were co-chairmen of groups, we had the invitations to further participants to come from them, and that is why I ask my question about who would have the confidence of many of you. Maybe you would just want to communicate further about that, but then the steps normally are that as the co-chairmen or the chairman constitute a group, then there are a series of regular meetings. The Transition group met in either Washington or New York once a month, and they had rather good attendance. Bill Rogers and Cy Vance would send the invitations. But the staff does the staff work. You would instruct us to look for something that you felt essential and have readily at hand. So we provide the staff work.

DR. CRISPELL: Are you sure? You have some time to think about it on your airplane trips; write down some thoughts.

DR. DUVAL: I have 20 written down now.

MR. MEADOR: If I can suggest, one of the ways specifically you could be very helpful beyond all of the great ideas we have gotten here today is to send in these names of people you think would make good commission members.

DR. CRISPELL: And we would love to have your ideas. We have heard other people's ideas and one or two pages of what the next step would be whether the intermediate step is what I'm going to call it between the president's physician and the vice president.

DR. DUVAL: I would suggest that in your capacity as director of the Center, you appoint a national associate who is a physician.

MR. THOMPSON: That is a weakness, that's right.

DR. CRISPELL: Well, as chairman, I always stop a meeting a half an hour before it is supposed to stop.

CHAPTER TWO

Summary of the Washington Meeting*

KENNETH R. CRISPELL, M.D., EDITOR

1. The President's physician was *not* involved in any decision re: the President's health and the need to invoke the Twenty-fifth Amendment when the President was shot.

    a. All decisions re: invoking the Twenty-fifth Amendment were made by the White House staff.

    b. Dr. Ruge was asked to meet with White House staff and the Cabinet on the morning following the meeting–he reported that the President was *alert* and able to function.

2. The M.D. Committee felt that the President's physician should be more involved in decisions regarding the President's health and the ability or inability of the President to function.

    a. The decision should not be his alone, but he should have an *official* consulting team.

    b. One suggestion was the:

        1. President–American College of Physicians

From a memorandum written to Professors Daniel J. Meador, Kenneth W. Thompson, and Paul B. Stephan III by Dr. Kenneth R. Crispell to summarize the pre-Commission Meeting of 10 October 1985 on the Twenty-fifth Amendment.

      2.   President—American College of Surgeons

      3.   President—AMA

  c.   For continuity we could suggest a six-member team to include the President-elect as well as President.

  d.   All felt that the Vice President needs a committee of physicians to advise him on the health of the President.

3.   The Committee felt that it would be best for President's physician to be a civilian and not a military officer.

4.   Norm Knorr's point about brain or mental function is a key issue. The question is whether a physical illness impairs mental function—the ability to communicate and render judgment.

5.   Dr. Cannon suggested that we ask Dan Ruge to draft a job description of the President's physician.

6.   What is the next step?

  a.   Try to appoint a commission as soon as possible. Mortimer Caplin is willing to help and might consider being co-chairman.

  b.   How many physicians should be on the commission?

  c.   William Spong has shown interest in the subject and I believe would serve.

  d.   Do we need to consider "or some other body as Congress may appoint"?

  e.   Should and can we involve President Ford and President Carter?

  f.   Would Vice President Mondale be of any help?

Kenneth R. Crispell, M.D., Editor

November 5, 1985

MEMORANDUM[*]

TO: Professors Kenneth Crispell, Kenneth Thompson, and
        Paul Stephan

FROM: Daniel J. Meador

RE: Miller Center Twenty-fifth Amendment Project

    I am writing this memorandum as a means of putting down on
paper some tentative thoughts I have about matters that should be
focused on in this project and that should be dealt with in the
Commission's final report. I am doing this so as to not lose track
of some of my own thinking and also as a list of suggestions for
Paul Stephan to consider in preparing a discussion paper for the use
of Commission members when they are designated.

The Physician to the President

    After reflecting on our meeting with Dr. Daniel Ruge I have
become increasingly convinced that the physician to the President
is a key figure insofar as invocation of the Twenty-fifth Amendment
is concerned. Therefore, I think that this position should be
considered carefully by the Commission, and the Commission report
should contain a significant segment on this subject. For example,
the report might describe the role of this physician, the type of
person ideally suited to fill it, and the responsibilities that this
physician has to the President as his patient and to the country
through the Vice President and the Cabinet members. The report
might even undertake the ambitious task of specifically setting out
a "code of conduct" for the President's physician in order to

---

[*]*Reprinted by permission of Daniel J. Meador.*

71

attempt to legitimate this physician's departure under certain circumstances from the normal physician-patient relationship of confidentiality. We should definitely arrange to interview the physician to Presidents Carter and Ford, and we should prepare an edited transcript of the Ruge meeting for all of the Commission members.

Facilitating the Invocation of Section 3

The report should attempt to explain, as Senator Bayh put it, that invoking Section 3 of the Twenty-fifth Amendment is no "big deal." Its invocation should be made to appear to be a normal, routine act whenever the President is undergoing surgery or is simply sick. I believe that a major purpose to be served by this report is the education of the public and the politicians. This section of the report could be particularly helpful in placing this whole matter in a better light. The report should also undertake to prescribe standing procedures to be ready for emergencies. I am struck by the fact that the President is always accompanied by emergency medical equipment and is provided with instant access to the nuclear code. However, apparently no one has ever considered that he should also be accompanied by a means to invoke Section 3 of the Twenty-fifth Amendment immediately. I would suggest, for example, that the President always be accompanied by a letter addressed to the President pro tem and the Speaker of the House invoking Section 3 of the Twenty-fifth Amendment with space provided for dating and signing by the President. The person carrying the nuclear code could also carry this letter. It could be signed in a matter of seconds by the President even after being shot. For example, President Reagan could have signed such a ready-prepared letter after entering the emergency room at the hospital. The report might include the precise text of such a letter to be used as a form by future White House staff members.

Kenneth R. Crispell, M.D., Editor

The Peculiar Position of the Vice President and Procedures to Deal with It

The Vice President is in a delicate and peculiar position because any step taken by him to invoke Section 4 of the Twenty-fifth Amendment might be seen as usurpation or as indicating his judgment that the President is not up to it. The report should undertake to suggest procedures that could be incorporated into an Act of Congress that would, in effect, "take the Vice President off the hook." Such procedures might provide means whereby the Cabinet or the "other body" would initiate the matter and reach a judgment before bringing the Vice President into the process. I do not have these worked out in my mind, but I believe that this subject should receive careful attention. There were some good suggestions made about this in our meeting with Dr. Ruge.

The "Other Body"

The Commission should explore possibilities for congressional creation of a body other than the Cabinet for acting with the Vice President to determine presidential disability under Section 4. Senator Bayh thought that this provision is in Section 4 to take care of an emergency—to be employed only in the event that for some reason the Cabinet could not or would not function. During the hearings on the Bayh amendment, no suggestions for any body other than the Cabinet seemed to attract much support. That still may be the situation. However, I believe that the subject should be carefully considered.

Medical Advisers

The Commission should explore possibilities for using a panel of perhaps three highly competent physicians either to undertake periodic examinations of the President or to render their advice to the Vice President or the Cabinet under certain circumstances or when such advice is requested. This suggestion is directed to the problem that permeates much of the concern under the Twenty-fifth

73

Amendment as to how medical judgment and opinion can be integrated into the ultimate political judgment that must be made under Section 4.

The Meaning of "Unable"

In both Sections 3 and 4 the key words are "unable to discharge the powers and duties of his office." According to Senator Bayh and the records of the hearing on the Amendment, little attention was paid to the meaning of "unable." Most persons seem to think that this is ultimately a matter of political judgment. Yet surely such judgment involves a significant medical component. Whether it is feasible to set out any meaningful definition prospectively and in general is not yet clear to me. However, I think it would be worthwhile for the Commission to give some attention to this point and to attempt to say something in the report that could provide useful guidance to future Vice Presidents, Cabinet members, and President's physicians. For example, the report could speak to such questions as whether the concept includes impaired functioning as a result of medication, psychiatric disorder, and short-term impairments.

Proposals for Statutory Enactments

Two kinds of possible congressional enactments occur to me as deserving careful attention by the Commission:

1. A statute (already suggested above) that would speak out procedure for invoking Section 4 of the Twenty-fifth Amendment. In my opinion Congress has authority to specify the process through which the Vice President and the Cabinet (or other body) must act in order to bring into play Section 4—so long, as course, as the statutorily prescribed procedures are not inconsistent with the provisions of Section 4.

2. A revision of the presidential succession statute that was enacted in 1948. This at least ought to be considered,

even though it is not clear that agreement could be reached on what needs to be done with the existing statute. At the very least, we should be sure that the existing statute meshes neatly with the provisions of the Twenty-fifth Amendment and the possibilities that might arise under it.

CHAPTER THREE

Meeting of the Medical Advisory Committee, Washington, D.C.*

KENNETH R. CRISPELL, M.D., CHAIRMAN

Issues which were discussed in some detail:

I.   The role of the President's physician.

      1.   When is his loyalty to the President usurped by the loyalty to the country?

      2.   Can we develop a code of professional conduct for the President's physician that would help clarify the ethical issues in breaking confidentiality? The President and the physician appointee should be made aware of and agree in writing to this code of conduct.

      3.   The President's physician should be an M.D. or D.O.

The meeting of the Medical Advisory Committee was held on 14 February 1986. Participants included Doctors Kenneth R. Crispell, Tom Connally, Merlin K. DuVal, John Hogness, Dan Ruge, and Roy Schwarz, and Professors Daniel J. Meador and Paul B. Stephan III.

4. The President's physician may be more effective and have less conflict of interest if a civilian rather than a member of the military.

5. The President's physician should play a *key* role in the decision of the President to assume the duties of the office if Section 3 has been invoked.

6. The diagnosis of "inability to serve" or "unable to discharge the duties" in most cases will probably be based on some type of medical disability—physical or mental.

   a. Historically the physicians to Wilson, Roosevelt, and Kennedy withheld medical information from the public, the White House staff, and the Cabinet.

   b. Under the Reagan administration it seems apparent that the White House staff made a political decision to invoke or not invoke either Section 3 or 4 with little or no input from the President's physician. At best this was true during the attempted assassination.

   c. Should we suggest the appointment of a statutory panel of three physicians to assist the President's physician and also be directly available to the Vice President and/or the Cabinet to assist in the determination of "inability to serve"?

II. Section 3

1. Can we develop a series of guidelines that would require the President to invoke Section 3?

   a. E.g., prolonged surgery, anesthesia, and a recovery period of 24 hours.

   b. E.g., a heart attack requiring the use of the intensive care unit and oxygen therapy.

    c. E.g., any medical situation in which the state of normal consciousness would be altered for 48 hours.

III. Section 4

    1. Is there a method of guaranteeing a medical input into the decision process?

    2. Should we suggest an alternate method or the formation of a statutory body to employ the Vice President and/or the Cabinet to initiate Section 4?

IV. The Diagnosis of Inability to Serve in most cases will be based on physical or mental incompetence.

V. The decision to use or not use this medical information will undoubtedly be political!

VI. Richard Longaker summarized the situation as follows:

> In sum, each case of presidential inability will impose its own set of imperatives and inhibitions on the President and the Vice President alike. Among the many variables in each case will be the relative urgency of international and domestic problems, the ambition and self-restraint of the political actors, and the nature of the President's inability. In a word, the amendment is only technically self-executing. Nonetheless, it contains all that a constitutional device should: a set of presumptions about the process of exercising power and an implicit expectation that it will be applied in a mood of restraint.

CHAPTER FOUR

Proposal for a Study Commission on the Disability of the President*

KENNETH R. CRISPELL, M.D., EDITOR

Introduction

On 6 July 1965, the Congress of the United States approved the Twenty-fifth Amendment to the Constitution, which was subsequently ratified by the necessary three-fourths of the states on 10 February 1967. The impetus for the Amendment, which deals with the succession of the President in case of death or disability, was generated in the wake of President Kennedy's assassination in 1963. The substance of the Amendment deals with the devolution of the powers of the Office of the President: Who is constitutionally mandated to be the Chief Executive of the country in case of illness or death? In the case of sudden, unforeseen death—such as assassination—the dictates of the Amendment are clear. Power passes immediately from the President to the Vice President, then to the Speaker of the House, then to the President pro tempore of the Senate, and so on. The line of succession is distinct and unequivocal in this case. However, in cases of what the Amendment writers call "inability," we find their intent ambiguous. We cite the relevant portion of the Amendment below:

Printed with the permission of Dr. Kenneth R. Crispell.

Section 3. Whenever the President transmits to the President pro tempore of the Senate and the Speaker of the House of Representatives his written declaration that he is unable to discharge the powers and duties of his office, and until he transmits to them a written declaration to the contrary, such powers and duties shall be discharged by the Vice President as Acting President.

Section 4. Whenever the Vice President and a majority of either the principal officers of the executive departments or of such other body as Congress may by law provide, transmit to the President pro tempore of the Senate and the Speaker of the House of Representatives their written declaration that the President is unable to discharge the powers and duties of his office, the Vice President shall immediately assume the powers and duties of the office as Acting President.

Thereafter, when the President transmits to the President pro tempore of the Senate and the Speaker of the House of Representatives his written declaration that no inability exists, he shall resume the powers and duties of his office unless the Vice President and a majority of either the principal officers of the executive department or of such other body as Congress may by law provide, transmit within four days to the President pro tempore of the Senate and the Speaker of the House of Representatives their written declaration that the President is unable to discharge the powers and duties of his office. Thereupon Congress shall decide the issue, assembling within forty-eight hours for that purpose if not in session. If the Congress within twenty-one days after receipt of the latter written declaration, or, if Congress is not in session within twenty-one days after Congress is required to assemble, determines by two-thirds vote of both Houses that the President is unable to discharge the powers and duties of his office, the Vice President shall continue to discharge the same as Acting President;

otherwise, the President shall resume the powers and duties of his office.

On the surface, the Amendment appears to be a work of sober and judicious reasoning. It provides for a methodical and legal transfer of power in case of the President's "inability to discharge his duties." Yet while the Amendment may be theoretically elegant and precise, we find it fraught with problems when one imagines it applied to potential crises. For example, what did the writers of the Amendment mean by "inability to discharge his duties"? Does it refer specifically to illness? If so, what type of illness? Are psychiatric and organic illnesses considered on the same plane? Moreover, if in fact an "inability" does exist, who testifies to the inability? Is the President's doctor, who would have the keenest insight into the matter, be required to break confidence with his patient and testify? How would laymen (who comprise the bulk of congressional legislators) evaluate a medical opinion if one were tendered?

We also find the time required to reach a decision should an instance of "presidential inability" occur to be intolerable. Should the President decide to challenge a Cabinet decision to remove him from office because of "inability," the Amendment provides for a full three weeks before Congress has to rule on the matter. During this time, the Vice President assumes the Executive's powers as Acting President, but the former Chief Executive still retains the title of President. In case of a grave crisis or emergency, to whom would the public and the governmental institutions respond, the Acting President or the President? Moreover, should Congress decide to uphold a Cabinet decision to relieve the President of his duties, the Amendment imposes no limitation on the number of times the President may challenge the decision. Conceivably, a President removed from office because of "inability" could continue to challenge the decision for the duration of the term to which he was elected. Apart from whatever domestic problems this type of situation might create, we would think it next to impossible to conduct a coherent, purposeful foreign policy. Governments around the world would be wary of making commitment to a President (or Acting President) who might be divested of power at any moment.

Not only would foreign policy initiatives on our part probably be stymied, but this "crisis of command" might well invite aggressor nations to take hostile actions against the United States in the belief that the executive branch would be unable to respond quickly and decisively.

In our nuclear age, it is this last possibility that most concerns us. In case of an ambiguous or delayed transfer of power, who controls the U.S. nuclear arsenal? Or, less apocalyptically, who is fully the commander in chief of the U.S. armed forces? Until the end of World War II, one might have supposed that even a delay of several weeks in transference of command could be tolerated. Current events, however, tend to move at dizzying speed and generally require some sort of instant response. How does the Twenty-fifth Amendment provide for this new reality in world politics? Let us take but one recent example to illustrate our point.

In March 1981, President Reagan was gunned down by a would-be assassin. From the time he was shot (approximately 2 p.m.) until he awoke the following morning after surgery, there was no formal transfer of command. The then-secretary of state, Alexander Haig, made an improper and ill-advised assertion that he was "in control" at the White House (and proceeded to misquote the Constitution). Later that afternoon, Secretary of Defense Caspar Weinberger informed Haig that the chain of military command passes from the President to the secretary of defense. At the same time, Vice President Bush, who would have assumed the presidency had Mr. Reagan died, was a thousand miles away at a political rally and did not arrive in Washington until late that same evening. Yet after he was installed in the White House, there was still no formal (or at least no public) transfer of command. Our question remains: Had some foreign power decided to act during the time between the shooting and Mr. Reagan's awakening in the recovery room at George Washington University Hospital, who would or could have acted? Was the military aide who carries the codes necessary to initiate a nuclear attack with the President or the Vice President? Given the direst of scenarios—an attack while Mr. Reagan was on the operating table—would the military aide have taken an order from the Vice President or some other Cabinet officer? And, lastly, even after Mr. Reagan was out of the recovery room, would he have been capable in his weakened and drugged condition to make any decisions of global import?

The hypothetical scenario that we postulate is, admittedly, a bit extreme. Defenders of the current system will assert that the current mechanisms worked well. During Mr. Reagan's recovery period, the government functioned smoothly; there was no overt attempt to destabilize the government, and (so far as we know) no foreign power exploited the situation to their advantage. The fact that nothing dramatically catastrophic occurred during this period leaves us unconvinced as to the merits of the system. We think that the United States was more fortunate than prudent.

Background

For the past two years, we have been preparing a manuscript in which we document situations in which illness in presidents affected their decision-making powers. By and large, these instances of malady in the White House have gone unnoticed, or when noticed, uncommented upon. The most dramatic example in the 20th century was the case of President Wilson's stroke while in office. Despite his demonstrable incompetence to discharge his duties, he lingered in office, paralyzed and semi-comatose, while the affairs of state ground to a halt. His domestic agenda was effectively scuttled; his plans for peace based on a sort of global parliamentary justice were doomed. Yet even while the keenest of observers was well aware of the situation, there was no formal mechanism in the Constitution to remove him, other than by impeachment, which, given the situation, would have been next to impossible to execute.

Twenty years later, a dying Franklin Roosevelt was sworn into office for an unprecedented fourth term. Wartime censorship, along with the concerted efforts of his doctors and aides, kept the full truth of his medical condition from the public. Since 1940, he had been diagnosed as having both systolic and diastolic hypertension, an alarming condition for a man of his age and in his position of stressful responsibility. By late 1943, he was suffering from the first signs of congestive heart failure; that is, chronic fatigue, persistent vulnerability to respiratory infections, anoxia (lack of oxygen), as well as periodic episodes of head and chest pains. By March 1944, his condition worsened acutely, and he had to be put on digitalis and prescribed to take bed rest to recover. Yet in the fall of 1944 (despite the fact that his condition had not improved), he was reelected. By February 1945 he was so weak and dissipated that he was barely able to handle more than a few hours of work within the confines of the White House. And yet, it was at this precise moment in history that he had to travel to Yalta, thousands of miles away, to conduct delicate negotiations with Winston Churchill and Joseph Stalin over the future of postwar Europe. Within two months after the end of these negotiations and less than three months into his term, he was dead.

We cite just two of the more dramatic and well-documented episodes we have researched to demonstrate that the possibility of a slowly dying President, whose lingering illness can sap his strength and cloud his judgment, is not a fanciful idea, nor would it necessarily have to be the result of an assassin's bullet. Presidents are as susceptible to illness as the man on the street, perhaps more so, but the effect that these illnesses have on the course of history is of consequence.

The Study Commission

Our purpose in proposing this study is to discuss this topic within the context of presidential succession. There are other problems that arise in the case of presidential disability, but we purposely limit ourselves to the Twenty-fifth Amendment to give the question coherence and focus. Because of the unique nature of the topic and its complexity, we would hope to draw together an interdisciplinary group comprised of the following list of specialists who would deal with the following questions:

A. Physicians

    1. What is (or ought to be) the nature of the doctor/patient relationship when the patient's illness

might affect the lives of others because of poor judgment?

2. Under what circumstances (if any) should a physician break confidence?

3. How does a physician dealing with a sick politician delineate between clinical judgment and political judgment?

4. If the President's physician feels the need to report that the President is disabled, whom does he contact?

B. Constitutional Lawyers

1. What was the intent of the writers of the Twenty-fifth Amendment in adding the "inability" clause?

2. How was "inability" originally interpreted?

3. How is "inability" currently interpreted?

4. How often may a divested President challenge a congressional ruling on disability?

C. Military Expert

1. Does the officer with the nuclear codes ever take commands from anyone other than the President? If so, under what circumstances?

2. What happens (or what has happened) when a President has been under anesthesia or has been comatose? Who assumes *immediate* command?

3. In a related circumstance, from whom, other than the captain, does the weapons officer abroad a Trident nuclear submarine take orders? Can the captain ever make a unilateral decision in case of presidential disability?

4. If a White House physician happens to be drawn from the military (as has been the case until just recently),

does military law govern his conduct? That is to say, in the military, a physician is legally bound to report any illness that might impair the judgment or impede with the performance of either an enlisted man or an officer. Does the President, as commander in chief, qualify as a military officer?

D. White House Aide

1. During the various times that the United States has gone into military alert, what has been the procedure at the White House? For example, what happened in 1973 when Mr. Nixon ordered a strategic alert over Soviet interference in the Arab-Israeli Yom Kippur war?

2. Who assumed the day-to-day command of the executive branch during the times when the President was incapacitated (e.g., when Mr. Eisenhower suffered his heart attack)?

E. Journalists

1. What should or should not be reported publicly about a President's illness?

2. Under what circumstances would an editor suppress a story about a presidential disability? Have there been previous instances in which such self-censorship occurred?

F. Ethicists

1. Apart from the legal tangles involved, what *ought* the principals dealing with this sort of situation do? If the law is ambiguous or counterproductive, should a doctor, for example, contravene the rules?

2. What import should be given to the time-honored principles of promise-keeping and confidentiality in cases such as this one? Does one have a right (or

perhaps a duty) to betray a patient's trust when the larger public welfare is at stake?

G.   General

1.   Who decides if the "disabled" President is still more capable of making major decisions than a healthy Vice President?

2.   Will it make any difference to the voting public if they know the candidate is ill and might become disabled while in office?

The questions involved are admittedly broad and overlapping, but we see no way of avoiding them without making this sort of exercise reductive. We see this problem as serious enough to merit the attention and study of scholars, politicians, and other leaders, and believe that no one discipline has the complete expertise to come up with an adequate solution.

We would hope to gather these specialists for the Study Commission under the leadership of the White Burkett Miller Center of Public Affairs at the University of Virginia for the study of the presidency. A more complete list of case studies and relevant legal and medical materials would be made available to the participants before they came. The ensuing discussions and debates would be "off-the-record" to allow for as much candor as possible. However, we would also like to summarize and edit the gist of the proceedings (with the participants' permission) to further the debate on this topic.

II.

PERSPECTIVES ON THE PRESIDENTIAL PHYSICIAN

CHAPTER FIVE

The Physician to the President*

KENNETH R. CRISPELL, M.D.

General

Dr. Daniel Ruge, physician to President Reagan, stated that "despite its glamorous name, the office of the White House physician is somewhat blue collar." It carries no job description and has only the powers implied from its entry as a line item in the budget. Ruge further states, "The job is so lacking in opportunities for creativity and medical skills that most physicians would shy away from it." Dr. Ruge and Dr. William Lukash (who served under four presidents) both stated that the general requirements for the job would seem to call for a senior physician whose reputation has been made and who is wiling to serve in the public interest. The doctor is in the position of facing two alternatives in case of presidential disability: either revealing the President's disability and unleashing the forces for medical removal of the chief executive or participating in a cover-up to keep the incapacitated President in office. Previous to President Eisenhower's illness there was a definite cover-up on the part of the physicians to Garfield, Wilson, and Roosevelt. These physicians chose doctor-patient confidentiality as their prime responsibility.

Printed with the permission of Dr. Kenneth R. Crispell.

The key observer in the health watch is the White House physician. Through his unique combination of access and professional training, he should be among the first to notice any deterioration in the President's capacity to serve. Although the physician has implied constitutional responsibilities in the event of presidential disability, he works from a cramped ground floor office in the executive mansion—primarily dispensing aspirin for headaches—and in the pecking order ranks with the curator and the usher.

Drs. Ruge and Lukash both felt that it was time to recognize formally the White House physician's post for its responsibilities and to outline its powers. The doctor does not need the stature of a Cabinet officer, but the position should be strengthened. They both suggested that it might help to require Senate confirmation of the White House physician. The procedure would assure a minimum standard of competence and provide a formal congressional platform for the doctor in case disability became an issue. Under the current format, a recalcitrant President could invoke his right to executive privilege to muzzle the doctor. There is also precedent for confirmation of White House officers. The President's economic advisers and his budget directors are subject to congressional approval.

Former Attorney General Herbert Brownell, Jr., who served under President Eisenhower, says a written protocol involving the President, Vice President, and White House physician would be useful in the event of gradual disability. The protocol would provide guidelines for both the Vice President and the physician, either of whom might be hesitant to act without such authority. "Speed and certainty are the goals," says Brownell, who took charge of resolving the disability dilemma when Eisenhower suffered a heart attack in 1955. Once there is a suspicion of disability, the matter can be turned over to Congress to resolve as the Constitution defines. But the doctor must be permitted to act without the fear of being accused of a plot to oust the President. "The public supports the President to the exclusion of everyone else. The public would have to be shown—not by medical opinion alone, which would not be respected, but combined with a political opinion—that the President was unfit," Brownell says.

Kenneth R. Crispell, M.D.

Without a protocol or some guidelines to help the doctor and the Vice President trigger the disability machinery, it is likely that nothing would be done until the President's disability reached a dimension of national concern. If the disability were covered up, as in the Wilson and Roosevelt administrations, there would be no speedy and certain resolution. The disability issue would be shrouded in speculation.

Former senator Birch Bayh in a personal interview echoed Mr. Brownell's thoughts about presidential power and the political question of disability.

> The thing that comes through is that there is nothing quite like presidential power. Some people will almost kill to get it and some will almost kill to keep it. Historically—here again this becomes a larger problem, I think, when you get into the disability discussion—the question is not so much a medical question as a political one.

Senator Bayh gave further insight into the method proposed by Mr. Brownell.

> It is only natural, I assume, that people around the President would think in terms of a President who was shot, killed, or almost killed. However, it is unwise if that is the only contingency that they plan for. It is a difficult thing to sit down and talk with the President of the United States and say, 'Mr. President, you know somebody might shoot you or you might have a heart attack.' That's a very difficult kind of thing to discuss, but I think it should be discussed. I had thought that starting with Eisenhower that had been a matter that had been discussed at the beginning of each administration, but apparently it was not the case.

The question of how to determine the inability of the President to "carry out the power and duties of the office" has been discussed off and on since the constitutional convention. It received a great deal of discussion during and following President Eisenhower's series of illnesses. In 1957 President Truman proposed that when a President is stricken with an illness, there should come into being a Committee of Seven composed of representatives of the three branches of the government. This committee would select a board of leading medical authorities drawn from top medical schools of the nation. This medical board, thus chosen, would then make the necessary examinations, presenting their findings to the Committee of Seven. Should the findings of the medical board indicate that the President was unable to perform his duties and that he is in fact truly incapacitated and not merely stricken with a transitory illness, then the Committee of Seven would so inform the Congress. Congress would then have the right to act and by a two-thirds vote of the full membership declare the Vice President as President. This proposal would hardly assure swift and decisive action.

A group of distinguished physicians, including Dr. Ruge, were convened to discuss in some detail the problems of the President's physician with particular emphasis on the confidentiality of the doctor-patient relationship versus the responsibility of the President's physician to society. No answers were provided, but it was pointed out that in 1957, the AMA council adopted the following statement:

> A physician may not reveal the confidences entrusted to him in the course of medical attendance, or the deficiencies he may observe in the character of patients, unless he is required to do so by law or unless it becomes necessary in order to protect the individual *or the community.*

There was also an in-depth discussion by the physician group of the Truman concept of a "Committee of Seven" or some such advisory committee. The general concept was that it would officially "protect" the President's physician but would probably prevent or hinder a real doctor-patient relationship between the President and the White House physician.

At this writing the suggestion originally offered by Mr. Brownell appears to be one of the possible solutions. To repeat, Mr. Brownell suggested a written protocol involving the President, Vice President, and the White House physician. We suggest that it might be important to include the President's chief of staff and legal counsel. The protocol would provide guidelines for both Vice President and the physician, either of whom might be hesitant to act without such authority. This protocol would be initiated at the beginning of each administration.

Could such a protocol be made mandatory by an act of Congress? How far can Congress go in spelling out the mechanisms or procedures that must be followed in order to write a decision about disability?

Senator Bayh in an interview about this question stated:

> I think they could pass an act that would provide for procedures. The question is whether you go beyond the procedure and the procedure becomes substance. But, I think they could establish a procedural format to be followed. I guess what we were trying to do with the Twenty-fifth Amendment was find a way which would meet with public acceptance and then public officials, understanding that the public would accept it, would be willing to utilize it. In short, we wanted to find a way in which presidential disability would not become a matter of leprosy. Presidents get ill. That's particularly why we had that provision that was used by President Reagan. If a President recognizes he is ill and the people recognize that the President becomes ill and there is a ready way of disposing of this, it becomes less a major consequence when it happens. The stock market doesn't gyrate. The divisions aren't set and aborted. It's a matter of business as usual, which is the way I wished that President Reagan had approached this. I think that is a sure way of lessening any public reaction or concern.

Section 3

The use of Section 3 so that "it is business as usual" will depend primarily on the President and the White House staff. It is a political decision with no or minimal input by the White House physician—with or without consultation with other physicians.

One suggestion would be to establish ground rules for the use of Section 3 in the previously proposed protocol for disability.

1. Section 3 would have to be invoked if the President was to receive a combination of anesthesia and narcotics that had a mood-altering effect for a minimum of 24 hours, and longer if it is a major surgical procedure.

2. The President can not reassume power at his own request. This presents some serious problems as exemplified by the following news release by Karen Tumulty and Michael Wines of the *Los Angeles Times* on 20 December 1986:

> *Washington*—Despite earlier White House denials, President Reagan may have approved the first shipment of U.S. arms to Iran *while ill or under sedation, a condition that may have left him unable to recall his action later,* Attorney General Edwin Meese told the House Intelligence Committee yesterday, according to a committee member.
>
> That explanation lends additional credence to former national security adviser Robert McFarlane's contention that he received oral approval from Reagan for the deal.
>
> The U.S.-made arms were shipped to Iran by Israel, which would have been legally barred from selling them without presidential approval.
>
> "The explanation is that Reagan either was in the hospital or recovering," said Representative George Brown, Jr., D-Calif., the committee member. "He may have been under sedation . . . [Meese] gave the impression that it was a difficult time for the president."
>
> Reagan underwent surgery for colon cancer on July 13, 1985; the first arms shipment occurred the next month. Brown quoted Meese, who testified behind closed doors, as saying that the meeting between McFarlane and Reagan would have been private.
>
> Meese's testimony, as related by Brown, would be the first time an administration official has edged away from the White House insistence that Israel made the August 1985 shipment on its own, without

U.S. authorization. Israel has maintained that the shipment was approved.

The issue is crucial not only as a test of the veracity of McFarlane and administration officials, but also because an unauthorized shipment could be grounds for suspending U.S. aid to Israel.

Mr. Fielding told us in his interview that he and Donald Regan had been assured by the surgeon that the President was "OK." They therefore advised the President after very inadequate evaluation of cerebral function to reassume office, perhaps the best political decision but *very* wrong from a medical standpoint!

1. The immediate surgical results were "OK," but anesthesia, major surgery, and narcotics produce major metabolic changes, including brain abnormalities.

2. A White House physician with *full* knowledge of the Twenty-fifth Amendment and concern for his patient—the President and the country would have been in the best position to offer expert advice about the President's mental condition.

3. The proposed protocol if it included an in-depth meeting of Vice President, chief of staff, with the President's physician to discuss when the President was to reassume office might help to prevent another catastrophe.

In 1966 after Congress passed the Twenty-fifth Amendment and before it was ratified by all of the states, Professor Richard Longaker of UCLA made the following observations:

Each case of presidential inability will impose its own set of imperatives and inhibitions on the President and the Vice President alike. Among the many variables in each case will be the relative urgency of international and domestic problems, the ambition and self-restraint of the political actors, and the nature of the President's inability. In a word, the Amendment is only technically self-executing. Nonetheless, it contains all that a constitutional devise should: a set of presumptions about the process of exercising power and an implicit expectation that it will be applied in a mood of restraint. Once the Amendment is ratified a Vice President will know that he has a constitutional obligation to seek support if deterioration of the President's health threatens the political order. Moreover, a President will know that a temporary declaration of inability is an accepted condition under the Constitution and that if he so declares, a Vice President will be available during this period to exercise the executive prerogatives without drawing into question his constitutional authority. However difficult the Amendment may be to apply, its greatest service is in making at least this much certain.

Many of his predictions have become a reality in the last six years. There will be a division of opinion about the failure or success of the Reagan administration in the non-use of the Twenty-fifth Amendment. At least the concept was used and some of our citizens became aware of some of the problems in applying it if the "actors" choose their own version of maintaining or transferring the duties of the President.

It is assumed that "inability to serve" will be primarily a political issue based on accurate and adequate medical input. One way to insure the latter is to have a well-trained competent senior White House physician with a full knowledge of both the medical and political problems of the Twenty-fifth Amendment. He or she must realize that they are responsible not only for the care of the President but at times may be responsible for the "care of the country." The White House physician must have a well-defined and acceptable political route, such as the proposed protocol, to make his or her concern about the President's "inability to serve" known to the Vice President.

CHAPTER SIX

The Physicians to the President*

KENNETH R. CRISPELL, M.D., CARLOS GOMEZ, M.D., and KENNETH W. THOMPSON, CO-EDITORS

History reveals that by no means have all of our past presidents been in robust health, mentally or physically. To what extent their ill health has been or will be a factor in world history is an indeed intriguing question, but one difficult to document or predict. In the cases of President Wilson in the last term of his presidency and of President Roosevelt at Yalta, however, one surely can speculate that history might well have taken a different course if these men had been well. In 1969 Dr. Hugh L'Etang, a British-based physician, noted that in 60 years, six of America's ten presidents and 11 of Britain's 13 prime ministers had suffered more or less incapacitating illness, some of them at crucial times in their nation's history.

Instances of ill health of our presidents and the care they received have in many cases gone unnoticed, or when noticed, disregarded. We have previously detailed the illnesses of Wilson, Roosevelt, and Kennedy. We will give a brief medical history of these three men and then concentrate on the action of their physicians and the care the presidents received or did not receive.

Printed with the permissions of Kenneth R. Crispell, M.D., Carlos Gomez, M.D., and Kenneth W. Thompson.

The most dramatic example of an impaired president in American history in the 20th century is the case of Woodrow Wilson. Despite his demonstrable incompetence, due to a series of strokes, to discharge the duties of his office, he lingered in office, paralyzed and semicomatose, while affairs of state *ground to a halt*. His domestic agenda was effectively scuttled; his plans for peace, based on a sort of global parliamentary justice, were doomed. He was actually incompetent for over 180 days while the government *ground to a halt*.

Twenty-five years later a dying Franklin Roosevelt was sworn into office for an unprecedented fourth term as president. Wartime censorship along with concerted efforts by his physicians, family, and aides kept the full truth of his medical condition from the public eye. As early as 1930 Mr. Roosevelt was known to have alarmingly high blood pressure, a condition no doubt aggravated by the stressful responsibilities heaped upon a man of his age. By late 1943 he was exhibiting sure signs of a failing heart, including chronic fatigue, persistent respiratory infections, and shortness of breath, as well as transient episodes of head and chest pains. By March 1944 his condition had worsened so acutely that he was administered the heart stimulant digitalis and ordered to take bed rest. Yet in the fall of that year, Mr. Roosevelt was reelected for his fourth term as president, his health unimproved. By February 1945 he was so weak and dissipated that he was scarcely able to perform more than a few hours of work at a time, that strictly within the confines of the White House.

It was at precisely that moment in history that President Roosevelt traveled to Yalta to conduct together with Joseph Stalin and Winston Churchill the difficult negotiations that would dictate the future of postwar Europe. Within two months of these negotiations, less than four months into his fourth term, President Roosevelt was dead.

The little-known facts of President Kennedy's illness add another chapter to the problem of illness in the White House. Little was known to the public regarding the fact that he had been diagnosed as having Addison's disease even before he was elected to the House of Representatives in 1946. This condition, caused by destruction of the adrenal glands, is characterized by marked fatigue, severe lowering of blood pressure, and extreme weakness. If untreated, the disease results in coma, which leads rapidly to death. Previous to the advent of modern therapy, the disease was nearly always fatal. With proper treatment (cortisone) it is now possible for patients with this disease to lead a relatively normal life. Even when confirmation that Mr. Kennedy was the victim of Addison's disease was made public late in the presidential campaign, however, this confirmation was couched in misleading terms.

Before examining in detail the illness of each president and their physicians, it seems worthwhile to examine President Johnson's illness and his relationship with his physicians. After his first attack, he was hospitalized at Bethesda Naval Hospital. His physician was a young man by the name of Dr. William Hurst. Johnson became immediately attached to Dr. Hurst. This doctor-patient relationship continued after he left office until his death. Johnson became almost immobile for several months after his heart attack. Dr. Hurst, with help from Lady Bird, finally convinced him to become active.

Johnson had his second heart attack while visiting his daughter and son-in-law, Chuck Robb, who was in law school at the University of Virginia. Lady Bird quickly called Dr. Hurst to come and take care of her husband. He came to Charlottesville and took over the care of President Johnson. This is an excellent example of doctor-patient relationship. No attempt was made in this care to hide his illness from the public.

As the illnesses of each of these presidents were examined, we found that their physicians played a major role in hiding the seriousness of the illness from the public. For example, Admiral Grayson went to extreme lengths to hide President Wilson's illness from the Cabinet, the Congress, and the public. Only Mrs. Wilson knew the seriousness of the president's illness, and even she was not given the full facts. Nor would she divulge any. Admiral McIntyre was quite successful in keeping the seriousness of President Roosevelt's illness from the public, the Congress, and the Cabinet. Dr. Travell was the one who issued very misleading statements about the actual condition of then-Senator Kennedy.

These examples point out the fact that the confidentiality of the doctor-patient relationship is a powerful force in the maintenance of silence about the physical condition of the president—perhaps too powerful. This was the age before "investigative reporting" and the almost daily appearance of the president on television. Could it happen again? Perhaps, but not to the same degree as happened with President Wilson.

The ambiguities inherent in both the original Constitution and the Presidential Succession Act gave rise to uncertainties regarding who is to determine that a president was unable to exercise the duties and powers of his office, as well as when and how such inability was to be terminated. There was also a concern that once presidential powers were yielded, they were permanently forfeited.

Following an attack of ileitis and a stroke, President Eisenhower undertook to avoid potential problems by executing an agreement with Vice President Nixon concerning the temporary devolution of presidential authority in the event of Eisenhower's incapacity to exercise the powers and duties of the office. The agreement provided that the President would declare his own inability if he were able to do so. On the other hand, if the President was unable, the vice president would make this determination "after appropriate consultation." In either event, the vice president was to serve as acting president until such time as the President resumed the powers and duties of office by declaring his inability to be at an end.

President Kennedy continued this practice, specifying the Cabinet as the "appropriate" body for consultation. President Johnson, first with House Speaker McCormack and later with Vice President Humphrey, reached similar agreements.

The illness of President Eisenhower nonetheless stirred some constitutional experts to worry about the adequacy of the Constitution's mechanism for transfer of executive power when the chief executive was "unable to discharge" his duties. Congress began a series of hearings, but little was accomplished until the assassination of President Kennedy in 1963. A series of congressional hearings initiated by then–Senator Bayh resulted in the adoption of the Twenty-fifth Amendment in 1964 and final adoption by the states in 1967.

Kenneth R. Crispell, Carlos Gomez, and Kenneth W. Thompson

Section 3 of the Twenty-fifth Amendment addresses the question of a president *voluntarily* declaring his own inability to serve. This section gives a president the power to voluntarily declare his own inability, the unilateral power to declare both the beginning and end of such inability. The most troublesome cases of presidential inability are those when a president cannot or will not declare his own inability. Section 4 of the Twenty-fifth Amendment addresses this problem.

The vice president is essential to the procedure set forth in Section 4. Whom would the vice president and the officers of the Executive Department consult if they wish to determine if the president were unable to discharge his duties? The president's physician? He or she is probably one of the few persons that sees the president daily, either in or out of Washington. By the present ethical code of confidentiality of physician-patient relationship, however, it might be very difficult for the vice president to obtain information about the president's health.

While physicians for centuries have been taught to honor the concept of confidentiality so beautifully articulated in the fourth century (B.C.) by Hippocrates, the physician caring for the patient holding high office encounters ethical, moral, political, legal and personal problems to a degree not encountered in the care of patients who are not in the public eye. The concept of confidentiality was certainly embodied in the manner in which physicians to Wilson, Roosevelt, and Kennedy "protected" their famous patients.

Can we continue to honor such individualized compassion if the result is a potential threat to the lives of the entire population? We would surely hope that being "compassionate to human beings" would continue to be a hallmark of our society, but there are many public offices in which poor judgment by the occupant can affect the lives of many persons—none, of course, more important or more powerful than that of the presidency of the United States.

Before any change, though, questions should be raised about the competence and the willingness of the physician or a panel of physicians to judge whether or not a person is too ill to serve, or more specifically, whether the physical disability will impair judgment. It is this question of impaired judgment caused by illness that will be the most difficult to substantiate by any physician or group of physicians.

A key observer in the health watch is the White House physician. Through the unique combination of access and professional training, he or she should be among the first to notice any deterioration in the president's capacity to serve. The doctor is in the position of facing two alternatives in case of presidential disability: either revealing the president's disability and unleashing the forces for medical removal of the chief executive or participating in a cover-up to keep the incapacitated president in office.

In an interview with Dr. Daniel Ruge, a physician to President Reagan, he stated that "despite its glamorous name, the office of the White House physician is somewhat blue-collar." It carries no job description and has only the powers implied from its entry as a line item in the budget. This lack of power or failure to be consulted about the president's ability to function was exemplified during the attempted assassination of President Reagan followed by surgery.

In his book *Gambling with History*, Laurence Barrett describes a scenario that occurred within the first few hours after the shooting. Fred Fielding, legal counsel to the President, was in the White House with Haig, Defense Secretary Caspar Weinberger, and Treasury Secretary Regan. Presidential aides James Baker and Edwin Meese were also present originally but soon left for the hospital to be near the President. Fielding, who had an intimate knowledge of the Twenty-fifth Amendment, had hastily prepared the necessary documents in case either Section 3 or Section 4 of the amendment was to be used by the President or the vice president.

While still at the White House, writes Barrett, Baker and Meese "briefly discussed the possibility that Reagan might relinquish his powers temporarily (Section 3). *They quickly dismissed the idea.* If a military emergency demanding an instant decision while he was under anesthesia, the National Command Authority system provided the means for coping."

In the case of President Reagan, it is of interest that all of those very important decisions affecting the safety of the United States and even the world were carried out *without consulting the President's physician* as to the seriousness of the President's

106

condition. This was despite the fact that Dr. Daniel Ruge, the President's physician, was present at the shooting and accompanied the President to the George Washington Hospital emergency room. Once it was determined that the President had been seriously wounded, Dr. Ruge turned the minute-to-minute care of the President over to the surgical team of the hospital. However, he remained at the President's side during the diagnostic, surgical, and postoperative procedures.

In the interviews with Dr. Ruge he told us that he was not consulted by any member of the White House staff or the vice president until the morning following surgery. At approximately 7:30 a.m. he was asked by Baker to meet with the staff. He was also asked to meet with Vice President Bush and the Cabinet following his meeting with the staff. This he did, and the only questions asked had to do with the status of the President's health at that time. Dr. Ruge replied that the President had recovered from the anesthesia and his condition was stable. He was *not* asked if the President was in a satisfactory condition to function as president. Dr. Ruge told us that if he had been asked, he would have replied in the affirmative. He would have been concerned, however, if the President had been forced to make a major decision involving the safety of the country.

The White House staff understandably sees an important role for itself in assessing presidential disability. Key members of the staff and in particular the chief of staff and immediate associates are in continuous contact with the president. They consider themselves uniquely qualified in judging the president's capacity for exercising his powers and duties. They are conscious of their prerogatives, fearful of threats to the president's authority and cognizant of the high stakes of political power. The White House staff has the most to lose if and when the president relinquishes his powers. Particularly in some presidencies, the staff carries major responsibility for the details of administering and managing the presidency. Therefore, they may be inclined to overestimate their role in continuing the functions of the presidency when the president is disabled. Political scientists studying the presidency may contribute to this view by emphasizing that the White House staff does the business of government in the absence of the president.

We believe that however skillful and effective, no appointed group of White House aides can take the place of sound medical judgment in deciding when the president is able to function and has regained his powers of judgment.

This serious problem of the power of the White House staff making a "medical judgment" is exemplified by the following news release on 20 December 1986 written by Karen Tumulty and Michael Wines of the *Los Angeles Times*:

> *Washington*—Despite earlier White House denials, President Reagan may have approved the first shipment of U.S. arms to Iran *while ill or under sedation, a condition that may have left him unable to recall his action later*, Attorney General Edwin Meese told the House Intelligence Committee yesterday, according to a committee member.
>
> That explanation lends additional credence to former national security adviser Robert McFarlane's contention that he received oral approval from Reagan for the deal.
>
> The U.S.-made arms were shipped to Iran by Israel, which would have been legally barred from selling them without presidential approval.
>
> "The explanation is that Reagan either was in the hospital or recovering," said Representative George Brown, Jr., D-Calif., the committee member. "He may have been under sedation . . . (Meese) gave the impression that it was a difficult time for the president."
>
> Reagan underwent surgery for colon cancer on July 13, 1985; the first arms shipment occurred the next month. Brown quoted Meese, who testified behind closed doors, as saying that the meeting between McFarlane and Reagan would have been private.
>
> Meese's testimony, as related by Brown, would be the first time an administration official has edged away from the White House insistence that Israel made the August 1985 shipment on its own, without U.S. authorization. Israel has maintained that the shipment was approved.
>
> The issue is crucial not only as a test of the veracity of McFarlane and administration officials, but also because an unauthorized shipment could be grounds for suspending U.S. aid to Israel.

Mr. Fielding told us in his interview that he and Donald Regan had been assured by the surgeon that the President was "OK." They therefore advised the President to reassume office.

The immediate surgical results were "OK," but anesthesia, major surgery, and narcotics produce major metabolic changes, including brain abnormalities. A White House physician with *full* knowledge of the Twenty-fifth Amendment and concern for the patient—the president and the country would have been in the best position to offer expert advice about the president's mental condition.

Although not stated specifically, the Twenty-fifth Amendment places the president's physician in a potentially powerful political position. The president's physician cannot officially initiate the process of removing a disabled president. Although we fully understand that the removal is primarily a political process, the decision by the vice president and the Cabinet to initiate the proceedings will most likely be based on medical disability rather than political disability. If true, this places the president's physician(s) in a key position.

To further clarify the role of the president's physician(s), we interviewed Dr. William Lukash, who served four presidents: Johnson, Nixon, Ford, and Carter. He had thus been in office before and after the enactment of the Twenty-fifth Amendment. He was well acquainted with the amendment, as they were prepared to use Section 3 if and when President Carter would require anesthesia for contemplated surgery for hemorrhoids. The surgery was not necessary, so it became a moot question.

Dr. Lukash suggested that congressional approval might increase the importance of the position and provide more clout when dealing with the vice president, the Cabinet, and the White House. In recent correspondence Dr. Ruge expressed somewhat the same opinion as Dr. Lukash. Physicians to the president are not accorded the same recognition that they receive on the outside, nor the same accorded to other White House officials, so they lack clout.

It is to be noted that Dr. Lukash was a member of the Armed Services while serving the president. Dr. Ruge was in the Veterans Administration, in essence a civilian, when he assumed office.

Neither physician felt that the previous position was a necessity for carrying out the duties. Both pointed out, however, the advantages and disadvantages of civilian versus military background.

Dr. Ruge and Dr. Lukash both stated that the general requirements for the job would seem to call for a senior physician whose reputation has been made and who is willing to serve in the public interest. They felt that it is time to recognize formally the White House physician's post for its responsibilities and to outline its powers. The doctor does not need the stature of a Cabinet officer, but the position should be strengthened. They also suggested that it might help to require Senate confirmation of the White House physician. The procedure would assure a minimum standard of competence and provide a formal congressional platform for the doctor in case disability became an issue.

Former Attorney General Herbert Brownell, Jr., who served under President Eisenhower, says a written protocol involving the president, vice president, and White House physician would be useful in the event of disability. The protocol would provide guidelines for both the vice president and the physician, either of whom might be hesitant to act without such authority. "Speed and certainty are the goals," says Brownell, who took charge of resolving the disability dilemma when Eisenhower suffered a heart attack in 1955. Once there is a suspicion of disability, the matter can be turned over to Congress to resolve as the Constitution defines, but the doctor must be permitted to act without fear of being accused of a plot to oust the president.

"The public supports the president to the exclusion of everyone else. The public would have to be shown that the president was unfit," Brownell says. Without a protocol or some guidelines to help the doctor and the vice president trigger the disability machinery, it is likely that nothing would be done until the president's disability reached a dimension of national concern. If the disability were covered up, as in the Wilson and Roosevelt administrations, there would be no speedy and certain resolution. The disability issue would be shrouded in speculation.

Former senator Birch Bayh, the author of the Twenty-fifth Amendment, stated in a personal interview echoed Mr. Brownell's thoughts about presidential power and the political question of disability. "The thing that comes through is that there is nothing quite like presidential power. When you get into the disability discussion—the question is not so much a medical question as a political one."

Senator Bayh gave further insight into the method proposed by Mr. Brownell. "It is only natural, I assume, that people around the president would think in terms of a president who was shot, killed, or almost killed. However, it is unwise if that is the only contingency that they plan for. It is a difficult thing to sit down and talk with the President of the United States and say, 'Mr. President, you know somebody might shoot you or you might have a heart attack.' That's a very difficult kind of thing to discuss, but I think it should be discussed. I had thought that starting with Eisenhower that had been a matter that had been discussed at the beginning of each administration, but apparently it was not the case."

The question of how to determine the inability of the president to "carry out the power and duties of the office" has been discussed off and on since the constitutional convention. It received a great deal of discussion during and following President Eisenhower's series of illnesses.

In 1957 President Truman proposed that when a President is stricken with an illness, there should come into being a Committee of Seven composed of representatives of the three branches of the government. This committee would select a board of leading medical authorities drawn from top medical schools of the nation. This medical board, thus chosen, would then make the necessary examinations, presenting their findings to the Committee of Seven. Should the findings of the medical board indicate that the president is unable to perform his duties, and that he is, in fact, truly incapacitated and not merely stricken with a transitory illness, then the Committee of Seven would so inform the Congress. Congress would then have the right to act, and by a two-thirds vote of the full membership, declare the vice president as president. This proposal would hardly assure swift and decisive action.

A group of distinguished physicians, including Dr. Ruge, were convened to discuss in some detail the problems of the president's physician, with particular emphasis on the confidentiality of the doctor-patient relationship versus the responsibility of the president's physician to society. No answers were provided, but it was pointed out that the 1957 AMA Council adopted the following statement:

> A physician may not reveal the confidences entrusted to him in the course of medical attendance, or the deficiencies he may observe in the character of patients, unless he is required to do so by law or unless it becomes necessary in order to protect the individual *or the community.*

There was also an in-depth discussion by the physician group of the Truman concept of a Committee of Seven or some such advisory committee. The general concept was that it would officially "protect" the president's physician but would probably prevent or hinder a real doctor-patient relationship between the president and the White House physician.

At this writing the suggestion originally offered by Mr. Brownell appears to be one of the possible solutions. To repeat, Mr. Brownell suggested a written protocol involving the president, vice president, and the White House physician. We suggest that it might be important to include the president's chief of staff and legal counsel. The protocol would provide guidelines for both the vice president and the physician, either of whom might be hesitant to act without such authority. This protocol would be initiated at the beginning of each administration.

Could such a protocol be made mandatory by an act of Congress? How far can Congress go in spelling out the mechanisms or procedures that must be followed to write a decision about disability?

Senator Bayh in an interview about this question stated: "I think they could pass an act that would provide for procedures. The question is whether you go beyond the procedure and the procedure becomes substance. But, I think they could establish a procedural format to be followed. I guess what we were trying to do with the Twenty-fifth Amendment was find a way which would meet with public acceptance and then public officials, understanding that the public would accept it, would be willing to utilize it."

Kenneth R. Crispell, Carlos Gomez, and Kenneth W. Thompson

At the present time the use of Section 3 so that "it is business as usual" will depend primarily on the president and also the White House staff. To date, the use or nonuse has been a political decision with no minimal input by the White House physician—with or without consultation with other physicians.

One suggestion would be to establish ground rules for the use of Section 3 in the previously proposed protocol for disability.

1. Section 3 would have to be invoked if the president was to receive a combination of anesthesia and narcotics that had a mood-altering effect for a minimum of 24 hours and longer if it is a major surgical procedure.

2. The president can now reassume power at his own request. This presents some serious problems if the White House staff without consultation with the president's physician makes the decision.

3. A White House physician with *full* knowledge of the Twenty-fifth Amendment and concern for his patient— the president and the country should be in the best position to offer expert advice about the president's mental condition.

4. The proposed protocol, if it included an in-depth meeting of the vice president and chief of staff with the president's physician to discuss when the president was to reassume office might help to protect a president from being allowed to resume his office before completely recovering from a temporary but serious illness that affects judgment.

Possible guidelines or a protocol for *mandatory* use of Section 3 by the president was discussed by the commission in some detail. It was the consensus of the group that it might be sound from a medical standpoint but politically was unsound, the reasoning being that any restrictions on the use of Section 3 might deter the president from using it. It is the hope of the commission that future presidents will see the value of using this constitutional amendment that allows for "business as usual" during temporary incapacity of the president.

In 1966, after Congress passed the Twenty-fifth Amendment and before it was ratified by all of the states, Professor Richard Longer of UCLA made the following observations:

> Each case of presidential inability will impose its own set of imperatives and inhibitions on the President and the Vice President alike. Among the many variables in each case will be the relative urgency of international and domestic problems, the ambition and self-restraint of the political actors, and the nature of the President's inability. In a word, the Amendment is only technically self-executing. Nonetheless, it contains all that a constitutional device should: a set of presumptions about the process of exercising power and an implicit expectation that it will be applied in a mood of restraint. Once the Amendment is ratified a Vice President will know that he has a constitutional obligation to seek support if deterioration of the President's health threatens the political order. Moreover, a President will know that a temporary declaration of inability is an accepted condition under the Constitution and that if he so declares, a Vice President will be available during this period to exercise the executive prerogatives without drawing into question his constitutional authority. However difficult the Amendment may be to apply, its greatest service is in making at least this much certain.

Many of his predictions have become a reality in the last 30 years. There will be a division of opinion about the failure or success of the Reagan administration in the nonuse of the Twenty-fifth Amendment. At least the concept was used and some of our citizens became aware of some of the problems in applying it if the "actors" choose their own version of maintaining or transferring the duties of the president.

It is assumed that "inability to serve" will be primarily a political issue based on accurate and adequate medical input. One way to insure the latter is to have a well-trained competent senior White House physician with a full knowledge of both the medical and political problems of the Twenty-fifth Amendment. He or she must realize that they are responsible not only for the care of the president but at times may be responsible for the "care of the country." The White House physician must have, when needed, a well-defined and acceptable mechanism to make his or her concern about the president's "inability to serve" known to the vice president. This mechanism should be established at the beginning of each administration.

In view of the importance of the president's physician in evaluating presidential inability, we recommend that the following guidelines be adopted in defining the role of the presidential physician:

1. He or she is now selected and should continue to be selected by the president.

2. To be an effective personal physician, the time-honored concept of patient-doctor confidentiality must be in broad terms maintained.

3. A possible code conduct for the president's physician would include:

    a. From the beginning of his appointment, the physician must have a knowledge of the history, medical implications, and use of the Twenty-fifth Amendment.

    b. He or she should be familiar with the views of the American Medical Association Council on Medical Ethics regarding patient-doctor confidentiality and those instances when it can be departed from in the national interest.

    c. He or she should have an early meeting with the president regarding the use of the Twenty-fifth Amendment due to illness. The physician should also seek a meeting with the president, vice president, chief of staff, and legal counsel to the president to establish, if possible, a written protocol regarding the use of Section 3.

    d. He or she should possess the knowledge, humility, and the expertise to obtain consultation to insure the best medical care for the president. Dr. Daniel Ruge, who met with the physicians' committee, pointed out that the president's physician, because of his office, had easy access to any consultant or group of consultants that he wished to see concerning the president.

It is of interest that Burton Lee, President Bush's physician, carried out the recommendations offered by Mr. Brownell. He met with the President, first lady, vice president, and the chief legal counsel to outline an emergency plan if the President became ill and incompetent. Fortunately, it never had to be used during President Bush's four years in office.

The political and world situation, the power of the White House staff, and, most of all, the wishes of the president will always determine when and how Section 3 will be used. We urge that because of his or her unique ability that the president's physician play a major role in the decision to invoke Section 3 and most of all when the president should reassume office if the Twenty-fifth Amendment is used.

In an age of nuclear weapons, it is the uncertainty of presidential power that most concerns us. Until the end of World War II, one might have supposed that even a delay of several weeks in the transference of command—while debilitating—could be tolerated. Events today, however, tend to move at a dizzying speed and may require some sort of instant response from a "healthy" president.

CHAPTER SEVEN

The Precarious Role of the President's Physician*

BILL McALLISTER

When the Reagan White House listed its top 55 officials for the 1981 *Congressional Directory*, it placed the president's physician at No. 54—between the chief usher and the curator of White House artifacts.

President Reagan has changed doctors three times during his seven years in office but, according to a recent report by the University of Virginia's Commission on Presidential Disability, the prestige of the White House physician has remained shockingly low. In the current *Congressional Directory*, the White House physician is ranked No. 55 out of 79 positions.

Whether or not Ronald Reagan's physician has clout within the White House may seem a minor issue.

But for a man who on February 6 celebrated his 77th birthday, who is the oldest man to hold the presidency, who has had colon cancer develop undetected, who has undergone three major operations, and who was shot while in office, few issues can be as important as the quality of his medical care.

Despite the potentially important role White House physicians can play in determining whether a president is capable of continuing

---

Reprinted with the permission of Health, *a weekly journal of medicine published by the* Washington Post, *5 February 1988.*

in office, only rarely have presidential physicians moved to the center of Washington's political stage.

"They're the lowest guy on the totem pole," said Dr. Kenneth R. Crispell, a professor of medicine at Virginia and one of the consultants to the Commission on Presidential Disability.

"It's a crummy job," said Dr. Edward B. MacMahon, a Northern Virginia orthopedic surgeon and co-author of the recent book *Medical Cover-Ups in the White House*, which details a number of accounts of poor medical care given presidents from Andrew Jackson to Reagan.

Both MacMahon and the Virginia panel, which was convened to discuss the problems of a medically disabled president, agree that the central player in any scenario involving the president's health should be the White House physician.

But the president's doctor typically is not accorded enough respect within the White House to take charge in a medical crisis such as an assassination attempt or major illness, the panel said. "The commission has been shocked at the low rank and, sometimes, the low esteem accorded to the physician—and not just in the current administration," it said.

MacMahon, a clinical assistant professor at Georgetown University, has raised medical questions as well, saying Reagan's medical care has "ranged from top flight to questionable." Administration spokesmen declined to comment or provide an interview with the current White House physician.

The quality of care is not the only issue at stake. How much should the public know about the health of a president is also a major question. Sometimes the White House was "a model of candor," but other times it appeared White House doctors "were muzzled," MacMahon said in his book, co-authored with Washington writer Leonard Curry.

Their solution: Senate confirmation of the White House physician. MacMahon said such a step would boost the office's prestige and give Congress "one sure source of direct information about the president's health."

The University of Virginia panel, one of a number convened by the school's White Burkett Miller Center of Public Affairs to deal with presidential issues, rejected the notion that White House doctors be subject to congressional approval. The commission said that a president must have a close, personal relationship with his physician and the selection of that person should not be subject to "approval by any other body, medical or otherwise."

Yet the closed selection process raises concerns about presidential fitness. Who is to decide whether a president is medically able to do the job? The question strikes at the heart of the role of the White House physician. As MacMahon put it: "The whole issue is: Whom does the White House physician serve? The president or the public?"

Crispell called it a "Catch 22": The doctor owes his position—and his power—to a man he must be willing to declare incapable of exercising presidential power.

Dr. William Lukash, the former Navy doctor who held the White House job under four presidents, told the Virginia panel any White House physician must accept "a dual loyalty . . . He or she must consider that he or she, and all those physicians who assist from time to time, are responsible not only for the care of the chief executive but also for the 'care of the country.'"

Reagan's Care: Lingering Doubts

Public debate over presidential fitness may be just beginning on the campaign trail. The Virginia commission timed release of its report for the start of the presidential primaries in hopes of getting the next president to begin considering the question before he takes office.

MacMahon's book and one that Crispell will publish in May called "Hidden Illnesses in the White House," as well as lingering questions about the quality of medical care given Reagan, seem likely to keep the question alive.

In an interview, Lukash, who served presidents Johnson, Nixon, Ford, and Carter, spoke of growing concern among some doctors about "cronyism" in the selection of the White House physician. This, he said, might lead to Congress's establishing "some guidelines" for who can fill the position.

The cronyism charge is not a new one, but it resurfaced with the appointments of Reagan's first two doctors. Dr. Daniel Ruge, who served from 1981 to 1985, was a Veterans Administration neurosurgeon who had worked for Dr. Loyal Davis, Mrs. Reagan's stepfather. Dr. T. Burton Smith, in the White House from 1985 to 1986, was a semi-retired urologist who had cared for the President in California. Both appointments interrupted a tradition of having military physicians, typically surgeons or internists, care for the president.

A number of doctors, including Lukash, maintain that the White House is no place for a medical specialist or a civilian. To begin with, the position pays a civilian doctor $72,300 a year, hardly enough to lure most experienced physicians out of private practice.

Military doctors are paid according to their rank and experience in the service. For them, working in the White House is a prestige assignment, one that allows most to continue practicing at one of the area's military hospitals.

The demands of the job also require a physician who is a generalist, Lukash said.

"This is a position for a seasoned physician, someone who can deal with medical problems that can develop any time and anywhere and an internist is most qualified," said Lukash, now practicing in La Jolla, California.

Crispell described the ideal White House doctor as someone with an ability to quickly diagnose an illness, such as an emergency room specialist, and assign specialists with the appropriate skills for work on the president. "His great forte should be his judgment," said Crispell. "Knowing when the president is ill and when to call in the specialists."

The University of Virginia panel and MacMahon's book raise critical questions about the role—or lack of it—the White House physician played when Reagan was shot March 30, 1981, and during his cancer operation July 13, 1985.

To the dismay of the panel, it found that Ruge, former head of the VA's renowned spinal injury program, was not consulted by senior White House staffers about whether Reagan was capable of performing his duties when he was hospitalized after the shooting.

The doctor should have a good working relationship with the vice president, the panel said. But George Bush "didn't know who Ruge was," said Crispell.

Ruge left the White House seven months before Reagan's cancer operation, but he did not escape criticism over his attitude toward annual physician examinations or the failure to see that the president underwent tests which might have detected his colon cancer at an earlier stage.

At the time, Reagan had gone 2½ years without a complete physical because Ruge, the President said in 1984, "doesn't happen to be a believer in those . . . he doesn't think they're that essential."

Reagan underwent surgery for the cancer at Bethesda Naval Hospital on July 13, 1985. Smith, who served as the liaison between the medical team that conducted the operation and the White House, was criticized indirectly by the Virginia panel's report for failing to keep senior White House officials apprised of Reagan's medical condition. "Prior to the cancer surgery, the White House staff received inadequate medical information or chose to ignore the information it did receive," the commission said.

The cancer operation may have marked a turning point for the Reagans and their health care in Washington. In late 1986, Smith suddenly resigned and returned to California "to attend to pending family business," and Nancy Reagan, described by White House aides as distressed over the intimate details given the press after the cancer operation, ordered new rules for the President's doctors.

The rules went into effect when Reagan underwent his third major operation, prostate surgery, in January 1987. Nancy Reagan told the doctors she didn't want them talking to the press and called on a friend of her late father to help assemble the team of surgeons from the Mayo Clinic in Rochester, New York. They conducted the operation with their own equipment at Bethesda.

Since then, all disclosures about the President's and Mrs. Reagan's health have come through White House press spokesmen and details have been limited by comparison.

Shortly after the operation, Reagan had abandoned his practice of having a civilian doctor and named an Army surgeon, Dr. John E. Hutton, Jr., as his physician. Details of how the 56-year-old Hutton, described by the White House as a "noted nautical photographer" as well as an experienced vascular surgeon, was picked are limited.

Some White House insiders say that one of the most influential medical advisers to the Reagans remain Dr. Richard Davis of Philadelphia, a neurosurgeon and Nancy Reagan's stepbrother.

However Hutton was selected, he has managed to avoid the attention—and criticism—given his two civilian predecessors. He had worked with both, serving since 1984 as one of the three military doctors who are called assistant White House physicians. The lack of criticism may reflect the respect Hutton earned working in hospital emergency rooms, a position that some doctors say should have given him training in how to quickly diagnose any presidential ailment.

During Hutton's tenure, Reagan has also had several small skin cancers removed from his nose and, citing his doctor's advice, the President regularly wears a protective skin cream when he attends even brief outdoor ceremonies at the White House.

In addition to caring for the President and first lady, Hutton officially heads what is called the White House Medical Unit. It is part of the larger White House military office and includes a staff, based in the Old Executive Office Building, that typically includes three assistant physicians, assigned from the military services, and several nurses and enlisted health care workers also drawn from the military.

While their primary mission is to offer around-the-clock medical care for president and his family, the staff also provides emergency health care for the 1,500 employees in the White House compound, a task that MacMahon said consists mostly of "dispensing aspirin and the like to members of the White House staff."

Hutton also has a tiny office in the White House basement, which his predecessor Smith noted was squeezed alongside those of the florist and decorator.

History of Controversy

Concern over the president's health is hardly a new topic in Washington. According to MacMahon's book, controversy over the role of the physician is almost as old as the position itself. The administration of William McKinley was the first to employ a full-time White House physician.

Military doctors often had waited on previous presidents in addition to their other assignments, a practice that provided a protest from the Medical Association of the District of Columbia during Andrew Johnson's administration. The doctors apparently were troubled that moonlighting military doctors might be taking patients away from them.

James Polk was apparently the first president to invoke his power as commander in chief to use a military physician as his doctor, and the office, like most branches of the federal bureaucracy, seems to have grown since then, according to MacMahon's book.

Part of the office's problem, medical historians say, is that the White House physician often has played a role that has been only part medical. Sometimes as important has been their role as confidante and adviser to many chief executives. The results have not been all positive.

Rear Admiral Cary T. Grayson, Woodrow Wilson's physician and closest friend, helped orchestrate what MacMahon calls "the most celebrated cover-up of presidential disability in the history of the Republic." The doctor aided the efforts of Wilson's wife to hide the severe strokes that left Wilson an invalid in the final year of his presidency.

Army Major Robert M. O'Reilly, another White House physician, undertook an equally serious and secretive mission, arranging surgery on a tumor in Grover Cleveland's mouth that the doctors wrongly feared was cancerous. The operation, conducted on a yacht in Buzzard's Bay, New York, almost killed the President.

Those incidents stand out as exceptions. Most of the work of White House physicians is routine, if not dull. Ruge, who declined to be interviewed for this story, told the University of Virginia panel: "Despite its glamorous name, the office of the White House physician is somewhat blue-collar."

A major concern of the University of Virginia panel was the minor roles Reagan's first two doctors played when he was hospitalized. "It is now obvious that the presidential physician can, and must, play an increased role," the panel said.

Just how to redefine the job is not clear. As the panel conceded: "It is far easier to say that the physician's job should be upgraded than to suggest how to do it." The panel urged the next president to draft written guidelines spelling out the role the physician should play in determining when he is medically disabled and should invoke the Twenty-fifth Amendment. That amendment allows the president to pass power temporarily to the vice president.

The panel recommended that the president invoke the amendment whenever he goes under a general anesthesia, something Reagan's staff did not consider after the 1981 shooting.

During his cancer operation, he did delegate power to Bush but specifically said he was not basing the delegation on the amendment, a step that the panel said was the result of incorrect advice from his staff. The Virginia commission said that the President's advisers were wrong in their assumption that the Twenty-fifth Amendment did not apply to such a situation.

Moreover, they differed with White House officials, who said use of the amendment during Reagan's operation would have set a bad precedent. The panel said it would have set a healthy precedent by assuring the public that the White House has in place an orderly, routine procedure for passing power to the vice president during such circumstances.

The groups arguing for a more influential physician acknowledge their proposal could thrust the physician directly into some of the most sensitive debates at the White House, put him at odds with the president's own staff, and give him a direct and continuing relationship with the vice president.

Whatever the changes the next president makes, the office seemingly can only gain prestige. In the current ranking of the *Congressional Directory*, Hutton stands far behind the director of the Television Office, nipping at the heels of the director of correspondence, and just ahead of the national security assistant for Asian affairs.

III.

INTERVIEWS AND CORRESPONDENCE WITH MEDICAL, LEGAL, AND POLITICAL AUTHORITIES

CHAPTER EIGHT

Interviews by
Professor Daniel J. Meador
and Dr. Kenneth R. Crispell*

INTERVIEW WITH ATTORNEY GENERAL
EDWIN MEESE BY PROFESSOR DANIEL J. MEADOR

At a Brookings Institution interbranch seminar on the administration of justice in Williamsburg I happened to end up sitting beside Attorney General Meese at lunch on Sunday, March 10, 1985. Along the way in the conversation I mentioned the proposed project on the Twenty-fifth Amendment. We chatted about it a few minutes before something else interrupted.

First, you may be interested to know that he seems to have a favorable impression of the Miller Center and was aware of the transition study and the presidential press conference study. He did not express a clear view one way or the other as to what he thought of a proposed project on the Twenty-fifth Amendment. He did seem interested.

I asked him specifically whether there was any consideration given to invoking the Twenty-fifth Amendment when President Reagan was shot. He said that no consideration was given then to invoking it but that there was discussion about the possibility of invoking it at a later point. He thought that things were pretty well

---

Printed with the permissions of Kenneth R. Crispell, M.D., and Daniel J. Meador.

in hand at the White House. He said that his first step was to get Attorney General Smith and Defense Secretary Weinberger to the White House so that law enforcement and national defense were covered. No one knew at that point whether this was part of some generalized attack on the government or what might ensue; thus, he thought that law enforcement and national defense were the two most immediately important areas to have in hand. He commented that President Reagan was signing bills on the day following his surgery and that there was clearly no need to invoke the Twenty-fifth Amendment.

He seemed to think that as long as a vice president is in place the procedure provided for in the Twenty-fifth Amendment is probably adequate and workable. A difficulty could arise, however, if there were no vice president. For example, if that should occur now the choice facing the decisionmakers would be whether to turn the presidency over to Tip O'Neill.

About all I can say about this conversation is that the present attorney general has now been made aware that the Miller Center may undertake a project on this subject. I should add that he was not at all hostile about it, and I suspect that he would be cooperative at least to some extent.

INTERVIEW WITH SENATOR HUGH SCOTT
BY PROFESSOR DANIEL J. MEADOR

On Monday, March 11, 1985, I had lunch with Senator Hugh Scott in Washington and we discussed this proposed project. I explained briefly to him the background of the project and said that the Miller Center was in the early planning stage. I invited his suggestions as to the pertinent questions that might be addressed, persons who might be suitable members for a commission to be established by the Miller Center, and ideas as to possible alterations in the present legal arrangements concerning disability and the determination of it.

Daniel J. Meador

I found his responses concerning persons somewhat confusing in that it was not clear to me from one moment to the next whether he was suggesting persons we should consult in the planning stage of the project or persons who might ultimately be members of a commission to study the subject. He said that we should touch base with members of the House and Senate Judiciary Committees. Senator Strom Thurmond should be talked to. Senator Mathias would be a good man to see, as well as Senator Biden, the ranking minority member of the Senate Judiciary Committee. In the House, he thought that Chairman Rodino should be talked to. He also suggested that the key staff lawyers on the two committees be consulted. As I say, I am not clear on why or at what stage he thought these people should be talked to or whether he thought that some of them should possibly be members of the group to study the problem. He also suggested that Jim Wright, Majority Leader of the House, should be contacted.

In response to my specific question concerning persons in the media who might be brought into the study, he suggested MacNeil and Lehrer, Roger Mudd, David Brinkley, and Hugh Sidey (he says that Sidey is especially well balanced). As to White House press people, he mentioned George Reedy who served under LBJ. Scott seems to think well of Philip Buchen, legal counsel to President Ford. Among former members of the House of Representatives who might be particularly good in this he suggested Barber Conable, Richard Bolling, and Henry Reuss. He thought that Howard Baker would not be particularly good because he is running for president. He suggested that we should involve possibly a leader from business such as David Packard, who is widely respected. Perhaps the head of the AFL-CIO should also be involved. He mentioned also the president of the Ford Foundation. As I indicated above, however, I am not confident whether he was suggesting these as persons to serve on a commission or persons to be consulted in advance about the project or persons who might be designated by Congress to determine presidential disability.

I asked Senator Scott specifically about his ideas on whether he thought the Cabinet was the best group to make the disability determination or whether he thought some other group that could be designated by Congress would be better. As best I could under-

129

stand, he seemed to say that the Cabinet was probably a good group unless some special situation arose where Congress felt that it needed to take a hand in the matter or where some special political situation suggested some other group; in that event, Congress could then pass a statute designating another group to make the determination. In other words, I understand him to say that Congress should not by statute prescribe in general some group other than the Cabinet but should reserve such action for a special situation that might arise in the future and then create an ad hoc group for that special situation. Such a special group might be headed by the Chief Justice. He thinks that it almost certainly would have to include the Speaker of the House and the Majority and Minority Leaders in both houses. It probably should include some persons from outside the government.

Senator Scott said that at one time he was intimately familiar with the plans concerning a national chain of command because he had a "Q" clearance. He is generally aware that such a plan is still in effect. He said that when he was Minority Leader of the Senate and Mike Mansfield was Majority Leader they had an agreed-upon plan as to a procedure for calling the Senate into session in the event of an emergency and that there was a similar procedure worked out in the House of Representatives. He said that when Senator Ellender, president pro-tem of the Senate, died, he and Mike Mansfield agreed within a matter of a few hours on the new president pro-tem (Senator Eastland) without the necessity of convening the Senate or delaying the matter to any extent. Mansfield had urged Scott to cooperate in this so that the line of presidential succession would have no gaps in it.

I told Senator Scott that at some point, as the planning progressed for this project the Miller Center might want to call on him again for suggestions and advice. He said he would be happy to help at anytime and would be willing to come to Charlottesville if we so desired and if a mutually agreeable date could be worked out. At this point I see no special need to get him here in the near future, but he is someone worth keeping in mind for later consultation.

Kenneth R. Crispell

INTERVIEW WITH DR. LARRY ALTMAN
ON BEHALF OF DR. KENNETH CRISPELL

I. Introduction

Following the Medical Center Hour on the Health of Presidents, a discussion was held with panelists Dr. Oscar Thorup, Dr. Kenneth Crispell, Dr. Laurence Altman, and Carlos Gomez, student, U.Va. Medical School. Also in attendance were Professor Kenneth Thompson, Miller Center, and Lehman Ford. The purpose of the meeting was to sound out Dr. Altman on the organization of a Presidential Disability Commission.

II. Physician/Patient Confidentiality for VIPS

The consensus on confidentiality was that VIPS don't want disclosure because of the damaging *gossip* that ensures. Dr. Altman suggested more study of the use of aliases by VIPS (a topic with which Carlos Gomez is familiar, viz., FDR). Dr. Altman said that even though the practice may be justified on national security grounds, it is arguably fraudulent.

III. The Twenty-fifth Amendment

A. *Psychiatric Illnesses.* Carlos Gomez reminded the group that Congress's preparatory work on the Twenty-fifth Amendment failed to plum the depths of presidential psychiatric problems (thus, an area that might be addressed by the Presidential Disability Commission).

B. *Twenty-one Day Limit.* KRC stated that the commission should study the feasibility of shortening the twenty-one day maximum limit that Congress has to decide a presidential/vice presidential disagreement on presidential disability. KRC's concern was that a shorter time period would be better for national security reasons.

131

C.   *Military Command Succession.* Carlos Gomez said that he
and KRC did discuss military command questions and
succession scenarios with the Judge Advocate General's
Office. The JAG Corps wasn't talking, but the spokesman said that JAG had already addressed every contingency.

Carlos said that Birch Bayh and Larry Conrad would
have preferred a bifurcated treatment of presidential
power so that military command could easily devolve
during a presidential disability crisis. However, at the
time the Twenty-fifth Amendment was being considered,
Congress could only reasonably address a limited number
of issues.

KRC expressed his doubts that the Presidential
Disability Commission should delve into the military
command morass.

IV.   *Presidential Disability Commission*

Everyone agreed that although the Presidential Disability
Commission should have a diverse membership, *physicians* must
make a unique contribution because they had *no* opportunity to give
congressional testimony during the Bayh Committee hearings.
Professor Thompson added that the commission's work could be of
important precedential value in any future presidential disability
crisis.

INTERVIEW WITH DR. DANIEL RUGE
BY DR. KENNETH CRISPELL

Dr. Bland Cannon and I met with Dr. Ruge at his office in the
Veteran's Administration central office. After listening to our
reason for the interview, he was very forthright in providing information as to what happened during the hospitalization of President
Reagan as he remembered the situation.

132

He described in some detail the events before, during, and after the operation. From our standpoint, Dr. Ruge was quite positive in stating that the President was "quite alert and functioning" within 24 hours after the completion of surgery.

From the standpoint of our study, he *was not* consulted about the physical condition of the President by any member of the White House staff.

1. Dr. Ruge had not read the article on "What Happened to Ronnie" from Barrett's book, *Gambling with History*. We are sending him a copy, and he will comment as to its accuracy.

2. Our interpretation as of now is that the White House staff, primarily Richard Darman with Baker's concurrence, withheld the document prepared by Fielding. This document would have been the use of Section 4 of the Twenty-fifth Amendment. We need to ask Fielding if Section 4, in which the president voluntarily transmits his inability to serve and the vice president becomes acting president until the president regains his health, was considered.

3. The White House staff made a political decision not to use Section 3 with no input from the President's physician as to the seriousness of the President's physical condition.

4. Dr. Ruge was of the opinion that the nuclear code—"the football"—was in the hands of the secret service agent, Lieutenant Colonel Joseph Muratti, during the surgery. He has no information that it was delivered to any of the Cabinet, the vice president, or the White House staff.

Dr. Ruge's relationship with the Cabinet, White House staff, and the vice president:

1. He had no contact with Vice President Bush and was quite sure that Bush did not know who he was or what

he did. Mr. Bush and family were taken care of by Dr. Yubb, an osteopath, trained in family practice.

2. He knew Meese, Baker, and Deaver but had no "official" relationship with them.

3. The morning after the surgery he was asked by Baker to meet with the White House staff and by Bush to meet with the Cabinet. He was asked to report on the physician and mental condition of the President. This was the *first* and *only* time he was asked to meet with either group during his four-year stint at the White House.

Special support service for the President:

1. This unit is under the supervision of a deputy assistant to the President—at the present time this is Ed Hickey.

2. It includes the President's physician, the secret service, and other persons to be identified (by us) at a later date.

3. It is administratively under the Department of Defense.

4. This unit is especially trained to handle all situations when the President is to be away from the White House.

5. Dr. Ruge feels that the President's physician should be "more involved" in some way in decisions in which the health of the President is a major issue.

    a. He is well acquainted with the Twenty-fifth Amendment and of the issue "inability to serve."

    b. He has no specific recommendations at the moment. He is willing to meet with us and share some of his thoughts about possible changes that could be instituted.

General thoughts by Dr. Ruge about his position:

1. His *primary* duty was the care of his patient—the President.

2. He now realizes he was "part of history" during the Reagan shooting. However, he did not really think about it until several hours after the President's surgery.

3. He consciously maintained a low profile and believes that as it should be.

4. He thinks it is an advantage for the President's physician to be nonmilitary.

5. As the President's physician, he had the privilege of asking for consulting specialists in any field.

6. He stayed at George Washington Hospital with the President but turned over the actual medical care to the George Washington staff. This included having Dr. Dennis O'Leary make the announcements about the President's medical condition.

SUMMARY OF INTERVIEW WITH SENATOR BIRCH BAYH BY DR. KENNETH CRISPELL

A. Short resume of my concept of meeting with Senator Bayh.

1. His approach to the Twenty-fifth Amendment was an attempt to maintain *continuity* of government when the president was temporarily or permanently disabled—the vice president was elected by the people and was a logical choice to assume the office.

2. He desired a mechanism that forced the vice president to act in this situation so we would not have a repeat of the Wilson-Marshall fiasco.

3. He seemed to *assume* (previous to our discussion on Monday) that determining "inability" under Section 4 was relatively simple. I believe at the end of our discussion he was convinced that it was a serious problem for physicians and the vice president.

4.   He suggested that we in some way make the President's physician legally responsible for reporting to the vice president that the president was "unable to discharge the duties" of the office.

5.   He was well aware of the tremendous power of the White House staff in preventing the implementation of the Twenty-fifth Amendment.

6.   My impression is that one of the main issues that was of great concern to Bayh was to formulate an amendment that had safeguards which prevented a coup by the vice president to obtain the presidency. The health issue was secondary to this concept.

B.   Proposals for the next step.

    1.   Pick co-chairmen as soon as possible and obtain their help in selecting and securing the services of other members.

        a.   I have previously suggested Morty Caplin as one of the co-chairmen.

        b.   New names to consider might be Father Hesburgh and Thomas Watson. Could we get Walter Cronkite to make a personal visit? Edgar Shannon serves with him on the Williamsburg board.

    2.   I believe we need a major input from physicians. Could we have a blue-ribbon commission of national eminence and have an M.D. advisory committee that would prepare a report for the commission that would be part of the deliberations of the commission and be included in the final report?

    3.   I suggest that we contact and/or meet with the following as soon as possible:

        a.   Dr. William Lukash—physician to Ford and Carter

        b.   Fred Fielding

c.   Herbert Brownell—if he is still alive and well

d.   Justice Powell—he was instrumental in preparing the ABA report that formed the main basis for the Twenty-fifth Amendment.

4.   Are we at a stage to succinctly synthesize our present deliberations, which could serve as a document to present to potential commission members?

5.   Although I believe there is a sense of urgency in view of Mr. Reagan's cancer, we should not be forced into a report that is short of excellent.

6.   I will write to Dan Ruge and ask him to prepare an *ideal* job description of the president's physician. I will ask him to consider Bayh's thoughts on a method of forcing the president's physician to declare him "unable to serve."

INTERVIEW WITH FRED FIELDING
BY PROFESSOR DANIEL J. MEADOR

Last week I was in Washington for the annual meeting of the Association of American Law Schools. It had occurred to me that I would probably not be back in Washington again for at least several weeks and that this might be a good opportunity to chat with Fred Fielding about this proposed project. Accordingly, I contacted his office and made an appointment with him through his secretary. Thus on Friday, January 4, I went to his office and we talked for about half an hour.

I explained the background of the project and the early planning discussions that are taking place now. He manifested considerable interest and said that indeed he thinks that this is a worthwhile undertaking. My impression is that he will be cooperative. He thinks the project can be carried out without access to highly classified information because hypothetical situations can be posed that are exactly like those dealt with in the classified material.

Fielding is "Counsel to the President" and heads a staff of several lawyers housed in the West Wing of the White House and in the old executive office building next door. They have developed a substantial book of directions, spelling out precisely the steps to be taken by all concerned in the event of the disability of the president. This book is simply written so that any reasonably intelligent adult can follow it. One copy of the book is in Fielding's office and the other copy stays with the president at all times. This book starts with the assumption that the president is disabled (suddenly, I gather) and therefore does not address the question of *when* he becomes disabled or how that is determined or by whom.

There also apparently exists in writing a "national chain of command" governing the chain of command within the executive branch. This has been developed, and it exists wholly apart from the Twenty-fifth Amendment and the succession statute. I gather that it is directed solely toward military and national security matters.

I asked Fielding for suggestions as to persons with whom we should talk during the planning phase of this project in order to get information or ideas. He said that Mary Lawton would be one, and he knew that we had already talked with her (Mary Lawton was on Fielding's staff at the time President Reagan was shot). As to others, he said he would like to give the matter some thought and would jot down some names and send them along to me.

I then asked him for suggestions as to persons who might be good possibilities to serve on a commission that might be created. Again, he said that he would like to give the matter some thought. I asked about Howard Baker. In response, he said that this would not be a good idea because Baker is running for president, and he would be inhibited in dealing frankly with these questions. He said that any hint on Baker's part that there might be health problems concerning the president would be fatal to Baker. The one name that Fielding did mention as a possibility is William Safire. He thinks that Safire might be a good possibility in that he has been in the White House and knows how the White House functions (knowledge that Fielding thinks very important to a study of this sort); Safire, Fielding said, also has thought a lot about the Twenty-fifth Amendment problems in connection with writing his book, *Full*

Disclosure. He thinks Safire is also an extremely intelligent, perceptive person, although Fielding says that he does not always agree with him. Fielding said that he will likewise give thought to names for possible commission membership and will send them along later.

All in all, Fielding did seem genuinely interested in this project, although he was obviously proceeding very cautiously. If he follows up on what he says, he will be writing me in the near future with some suggestions, and I will pass those along. He did say that he would be willing to meet with us or any planning group within the next few months to explore the matter further. I told him that I thought that this would probably be desirable and that we would be in touch with him about that later.

CHAPTER NINE

Correspondence between Professor Meador and Fred Fielding, Counsel to President Reagan*

The White House
Washington

August 30, 1985

Dear Dan,

Thank you for your letter of August 8 requesting copies of the President's letters and any other public documents prepared in connection with the recent transfer of authority during the President's surgery. The only public documents are the letters, copies of which are enclosed.

As you and I discussed previously, my office had undertaken a review of the legislative history of the Twenty-fifth Amendment some time prior to the President's surgery. Despite uncertainties as to its applicability, the Amendment is always available at the discretion of the President; in light of all the circumstances, the President decided that a transfer of authority to Vice President

---

**Printed with the permission of Daniel J. Meador.*

Bush was appropriate in this instance. The letter transferring authority pursuant to Section 3 was drafted in such a manner as to avoid establishing (or at least questioning) a precedent with respect to any future brief periods of disability, when the surrounding circumstances may compel this or future presidents to reach a different conclusion on invocation of the Amendment.

In any event, the Miller Center now has considerably more grist for its mill on this question. I certainly hope not to be compelled to confront these issues again, but I am confident that the work of the Center will be of value to whomever must do so in the future.

I will be pleased to provide any information or recollection to the Project's participants, if it is deemed to be helpful to its work.

Sincerely,

Fred F. Fielding
Counsel to the President

The Honorable Daniel J. Meador
James Monroe Professor of Law
University of Virginia School of Law
Charlottesville, Virginia 22901

Daniel J. Meador

THE WHITE HOUSE

Office of the Press Secretary
(Bethesda, Maryland)

For Immediate Release   July 13, 1985

TEXT OF A LETTER FROM THE PRESIDENT
TO THE
PRESIDENT PRO TEMPORE OF THE SENATE
AND
SPEAKER OF THE HOUSE OF REPRESENTATIVES

Dear Mr. President (Mr. Speaker):

I am about to undergo surgery during which time I will be briefly and temporarily incapable of discharging the Constitutional powers and duties of the Office of the President of the United States.

After consultation with my Counsel and the Attorney General, I am mindful of the provisions of Section 3 of the Twenty-fifth Amendment to the Constitution and of the uncertainties of its application to such brief and temporary periods of incapacity. I do not believe that the drafters of this Amendment intended its application to situations such as the instant one.

Nevertheless, consistent with my long-standing arrangement with Vice President George Bush, and not intending to set a precedent binding anyone privileged to hold this Office in the future, I have determined and it is my intention and direction that Vice President George Bush shall discharge those powers and duties in my stead commencing with the administration of anesthesia to me in this instance.

I shall advise you and the Vice President when I determine that I am able to resume the discharge of the Constitutional powers and duties of this Office.

May God bless this Nation and us all.

Sincerely,

/S/ Ronald Reagan

THE WHITE HOUSE

Office of the Press Secretary
(Bethesda, Maryland)

For Immediate Release   July 13, 1985

TEXT OF A LETTER FROM THE PRESIDENT
TO THE
PRESIDENT PRO TEMPORE OF THE SENATE
AND
SPEAKER OF THE HOUSE OF REPRESENTATIVES

Dear Mr. President (Mr. Speaker):

Following up on my letter to you of this date, please be advised I am able to resume the discharge of the Constitutional powers and duties of the Office of the President of the United States. I have informed the Vice President of my determination and my resumption of those powers and duties.

Sincerely,

/S/ Ronald Reagan

WILEY, REIN & FIELDING

1776 K Street, N.W.
Washington, D.C. 20006

Fred F. Fielding
(202) 429-7320   November 10, 1996

Professor Daniel J. Meador
James Monroe Professor of Law
University of Virginia
School of Law
Charlottesville, VA 22901

Dear Dan:

Thank you for your letter of November 4 inquiring about the "contingency" notebook prepared to deal with situations where the Twenty-fifth Amendment may have to be invoked.

When I last saw it, the book contained no national security classification in regard to the Twenty-fifth Amendment materials. In any event, I do not have a copy to share with you; it is considered to be a Presidential paper and protected as such.

You may wish to raise your request with my successor, Peter J. Wallison. To be candid, however, I am not sure that a review of the notebook will be of significant value to the Commission, as its primary purpose was to restate the provisions and have drafts of correspondence needed in each instance.

It was good to hear from you. Please let me know if I can be of any additional assistance to the Miller Center or the Law School.

Sincerely,

Fred F. Fielding

Fred Fielding

EXCERPT FROM TESTIMONY BY FRED FIELDING TO THE MILLER CENTER COMMISSION ON PRESIDENTIAL DISABILITY AND THE TWENTY-FIFTH AMENDMENT*

Fred F. Fielding, then counsel to President Reagan, in his testimony to the Commission, said, in part, the following:

Let's go back to the week before the operation. We knew—some of us knew—and I forget when it became public, that the President was going to have his physical. We knew at the time that he was going to have a form of anaesthesia, to have the procedure that occurred on Friday, if I recall my dates correctly. He was operated on Saturday, got a procedure on Friday. What was going to happen was that there was a possibility that if something was found that they would have to instantly put the President under. I used that as an opportunity the preceding week to schedule a meeting with the President and the Vice President and Don Regan (then chief of staff). We sat in the Oval Office and we discussed the whole situation: the National Command Authority plus the President's desires on passage of power temporarily if he were suddenly temporarily incapacitated. . . .

The decision was obvious that unless something unexpected occurred on Friday there would be no need for the Twenty-fifth Amendment in any, shape, or form. But Don Regan called me down later afternoon on that Friday and said, "We've got some problems with the health exam." And we went through the whole drill—if you will—of what is to be done and where is the Vice President, what is the press to be advised and what is not to be told, and the normal procedures that you go through. One of the subjects obviously was the Twenty-fifth Amendment. I can tell you, and I think it is important for the sake of history, that when we left, no decision of a recommendation to the President had been made

*Reprinted from the *Report of the Miller Center Commission on Presidential Disability and the Twenty-fifth Amendment*, University Press of America (1988).

although we knew the procedures. I drafted basically two letters: One was a little fleshing out of the letter that was already in the book,[1] and the other was basically the letter the President actually [was] signed. I did that because I knew that there was reluctance on the part of the President to activate the Twenty-fifth Amendment for a "minor" procedure of short-term duration. . . .

I thought the President should have two options: One was very clear, that of exercise of the Twenty-fifth Amendment; and the other was a piece that would accomplish the activation of the Twenty-fifth Amendment but was more consistent with what I perceived to be the President's concerns. His concern mainly was that he didn't want to set a precedent for future presidents. But I can tell you in all candor there was no political reason why he didn't want to, which theoretically there could be as with someone who is having a power fight or whatever you would with their Vice President.

Next morning I sat down with the Chief of Staff at the hospital and we discussed this. I showed him the two drafts, the normal draft and the optional draft, and I don't think Don's mind was made up at that point, until that point, to be very honest. I think his mind was still open about it. We discussed it and then we went in and discussed it with the President in the hospital room. And he made his decision; he signed the optional paper. As it turned out, the doctor had predicted three hours for the operation. He wanted to get a little head start, so he started the anaesthesia earlier than he had told us he was going to start it because he wanted to give himself a little more time. So there probably was a period of time in there, although it was academic, a technical period of time when the President was out, and we had not called Vice President Bush.

Later that afternoon we asked to see the doctor. [The operation surgeon, not Dr. Ruge, the presidential physician.] We explained to him the Twenty-fifth Amendment, the implications of it. We explored it with him. I was asking questions about how you could know, what was the legitimate way to determine whether the President was capable, understanding, lucid, and that sort of thing. We hit upon several tests, one of which was that I said "I'm going to ask him to sign a letter. How about asking him to read the letter and understand it? Wouldn't that be evidence that he was lucid?" And he said, "Yep." We went in a little after seven to see him. He was joking with the nurses when we walked in. We had a conversation with him; we discussed the transfer of power. I handed him the letter and he picked it up and literally started to read it and his eyes were shutting and opening, and it was obviously going like this, like he was turning his eyes. And I thought, uh oh, and Don Regan and I looked at each other and decided that maybe we were a little premature. Then the President reminded us that he didn't have his glasses and he didn't have his contacts on and he couldn't read it. It had nothing to do with his consciousness at all. We read the letter to him; we discussed it with him. Don said something, in effect, "Now that you know what we are up to, Mr. President, maybe we'll come back in a couple of hours and ask you to sign it," when at that point the President said (this is not a full quote, but something to the effect), "Oh, heck no, I don't want you to wake me up later. I'll sign it now." So we decided he was lucid enough, certainly, to take it back.

My mind was that it should not be shorter than necessary or longer than required since this was the first exercise of the Amendment. I would have had no problem with going overnight with everything we knew and all the briefings that we had and all the strategic information we had. But in my mind, again, my own personal view was if you were comfortable with the President's condition, the sooner the better for any number of reasons. And certainly it was a very practical, political reason that the public out there needed reassurance the President was in fact really O.K., this wasn't a death-threatening situation, that . . . had come through the procedure and was lucid enough to take back the problems.

The worse thing in the world would have been to have him transfer—and this was the other thing we talked about—the power to the Vice President, take it back, and then later have to transfer it back again. So that was a factor in our thinking as well. We had to be reassured by the doctors that the probabilities of that to occur was law.

Our question was not was the man in discomfort. The question was whether he was lucid or whether he had the ability to carry on, not whether it was comfortable in the short term. When somebody asked whether the White House physician was in on the discussion, the answer was no. But I know that Don Regan talked to the doctor at that time and we had discussed the scenario with him the night before. It wasn't that the White House physician was excluded; it was that once we got into the surgery phase that we were dealing with the surgical team.

ENDNOTE

1. At another point Fielding said to the Commission:

    One of the things that I had my staff work on was a book, basically an emergency book. What do you do about *X, Y, Z,* events concerning the President's health? I state in all candor that was not completed on March 30. Early afternoon, and suddenly the President was shot and we all realized (a) it was an incident, (b) the President was shot, and (c) it was very serious. The stories were many; we ultimately ended up in the basement room.

    Everybody now is aware of the Twenty-fifth Amendment. To be very frank with you, that day, when I mentioned the Twenty-fifth Amendment, I could see eyes glazing over in some parts of the Cabinet. They didn't even know about the Twenty-fifth Amendment. It wasn't a full Cabinet meeting, it was whomever in the Cabinet could be notified, started drifting in and taking seats around the table.

    The book is now finished. Whenever I would travel with the President there are two copies. I would always carry a copy with me of the book. There was always one back in my office in the safe. The book basically is every situation you can imagine that has occurred to the president or the vice president: It is, for that matter, scenarios.

IV.

EXAMPLES OF MEMORANDA AND REPORTS

CHAPTER TEN

Memorandum to Dr. Kenneth Crispell From Dr. Carlos Gomez on an Interview with Mr. Lawrence Conrad*

1. I spoke with Mr. Conrad out in Indianapolis on Monday, March 19, 1984. He is the senior partner in a law firm in Indianapolis and is also one of the campaign chairmen for Walter Mondale's Indiana campaign.

2. Mr. Conrad was chief counsel to the Senate for Constitutional Amendments during the 1960s and was the chief of staff on Senator Birch Bayh's committee on the Twenty-fifth Amendment. As such, Mr. Conrad was responsible for the language and the implementation of the Twenty-fifth Amendment. Moreover, he was the one who set up all of the congressional testimony that was given in 1965 and 1966 when they were drawing up this amendment.

3. My interview with Mr. Conrad went extremely well. He was initially a little guarded about the nature of our topic and when I explained to him that we would not release any of our findings until after the November election, he relaxed noticeably. Mr. Conrad pointed out to me that the Twenty-fifth Amendment was written in response to President

---

Memorandum of 26 March 1984 printed with the permission of Dr. Kenneth R. Crispell.

Kennedy's assassination and that their initial concern was with the proper transfer of power after the Chief Executive died. He further pointed out that it was not until 1967 (when the Amendment was ratified by three-quarters of the states) that the line of succession went from the president, to the vice president, to the Speaker of the House, to the president pro tem of the Senate, to the secretary of state.

4.   The disability clause in the Twenty-fifth Amendment was almost an afterthought. The impetus for that portion of the amendment came with Mr. Eisenhower's heart attack and with Mr. Johnson's gall bladder operation. In fact, if Mr. Johnson had not been ill while in office, there probably would not have been an addendum to the amendment.

5.   Mr. Conrad said that as far as he is concerned, the Twenty-fifth Amendment works "for the most part." To support his statement, he said that the amendment had worked to perfection during the Watergate crisis. In other words, when Mr. Agnew was forced to resign, Mr. Nixon invoked the language of the Twenty-fifth Amendment to nominate then-Congressman Gerald Ford for the vice presidency. After a very quick series of hearings, Congress confirmed Mr. Ford as vice president according to the language of the Twenty-fifth Amendment. When Mr. Nixon subsequently resigned, the language of the Twenty-fifth Amendment was again invoked, and as soon as Mr. Nixon's date of resignation became effective, Vice President Ford was sworn in as President of the United States. Following President Ford's swearing-in ceremony, he (Mr. Ford) again invoked the language of the Twenty-fifth Amendment and nominated Governor Nelson Rockefeller for the vice presidency. Once again, Mr. Rockefeller was interviewed very briefly by Congress and was approved and sworn in by the Congress of the United States. The bottom line, as far as Mr. Conrad is concerned, is that this mechanism, i.e., the succession of power, works to perfection *when all of the principals in power are in good mental and physical state.* In other words, what the amendment

provides is for a legal, constitutional transfer of power that is fairly quick and fairly effective and leaves no room for ambiguity as to who should hold the office of president.

6. Regarding the question of physiological illness, Mr. Conrad was more tentative. As far as Mr. Conrad is concerned, those are situations in which only an executive order can make any difference. In other words, what he suggests is that the president, the vice president, the Speaker of the House, and the president pro tem of the Senate get together at the very beginning of a new presidency and agree on a document that would be duly sealed and notarized as to when and if the president would cede his office (even temporarily) to another member of his administration. There is a lot of historical precedent for this, as Mr. Conrad pointed out. Certainly Mr. Eisenhower and Mr. Nixon had worked out such an arrangement. We suspect, but are not sure, that President Johnson and Vice President Humphrey worked out this kind of arrangement. We have no details as to what if any arrangements President Nixon and Vice President Agnew worked out.

7. Mr. Conrad is under the impression that the second the president is incapacitated for whatever reason (bullet wound, anesthesia due to an operation, kidnapping, loss of radio communication, and so forth) that the military officer who controls the nuclear code should immediately go back to the White House and locate the vice president. Mr. Conrad suggested (but did not state explicitly) that there were probably two military officers who carried around identical nuclear codes. What he further suggested is that one of these people stays with the president at all times and the other person is either in the White House or traveling on a military plane in order to be available precisely in case such an emergency arises. Mr. Conrad suggested that we find out whether or not this military aide with the nuclear codes actually remained in the operating room with Mr. Reagan while Mr. Reagan was being operated on in March of 1981 following the assassination attempt. If in fact this was the

case—that is to say, if the military officer did remain in the operating room—then as far as Mr. Conrad is concerned, the military officer violated the protocol. As far as Mr. Conrad is concerned, that officer should have removed himself immediately from the operating room the second Mr. Reagan went under anesthesia, should have gone back to the White House, and should have found out where the vice president was.

8. The only situation in which Mr. Conrad believes that the Twenty-fifth Amendment is completely defective is in cases involving psychiatric impairment. He sees no workable unambiguous language that can be put into the Constitution of the United States to take care of a situation in which the president becomes psychotic. Mr. Conrad suggested that we read a book by Fletcher Knebel, *Knight of Camp David*, in which the story line is that the president begins to have psychotic episodes but they are not severe enough or consistent enough for any one person in the Cabinet to gather enough data to remove him from office. Mr. Conrad believes that the situation described in the Knebel book would be the most horrifying as far as the Twenty-fifth Amendment is concerned because it takes a three-fourths majority of the Cabinet officers plus the vote of the vice president to remove the president (at least temporarily) from office. Now Mr. Conrad did admit that it would have been possible under the Twenty-fifth Amendment to have had Mr. Nixon removed from office without an impeachment trial and conviction if, in fact, someone in the Cabinet had been willing to testify to the possibility (or to the fact) that Mr. Nixon was *non compus mentis*. The problem that I pointed out to Mr. Conrad is that all of Mr. Nixon's Cabinet officers at that point were his old cronies. None of them, insofar as we can tell from the records, was prepared to make any dramatic statement or any dramatic move against their own president. Therefore, one of the flaws of this amendment is that it requires that the very people in whom the president places the most trust be precisely the ones who would remove him from office. I told

him, and he agreed with me, that this was a very unlikely situation.

9. Another concern that Mr. Conrad had when I suggested that we were thinking about rewriting the amendment, was that the transfer of power in the presidency be something that would be very difficult to do. In other words, it should not be what he called "a political football." Mr. Conrad believes that the Executive Office, and particularly the office of the president, needs to be a very powerful, very stable institution in this country, and if we make it any weaker than it already is, he fears that it may be impossible to govern this country. He made the example of the parliamentary system in Great Britain or Israel, in which every time there is a crisis of confidence in the country, the prime minister has to call new elections and pull together an entirely new parliamentary majority. Mr. Conrad stated (and I think he is right) that a country like this one that has so much power at its disposal, and to whom so much of the world looks for stability and leadership, cannot afford to have the office of president bandied about with disregard.

10. Mr. Conrad went further in suggesting that the real problem with the Twenty-fifth Amendment (such as there is) is the nuclear question. He said, and I agree with him, that were this not the nuclear age, we could probably find a variety of mechanisms for dealing with this problem and not have it turn into a catastrophe. In fact, though, this is the nuclear age, and we live in a situation in which decisions affecting the course not only of history but of the very existence of the world have to be made not in a matter of days or even hours, but in a matter of minutes. Mr. Conrad suggested that an alternative way of attacking this problem would be to go through the Pentagon and see how much information we could find out on what kind of nuclear contingencies the Pentagon has set up in case of a nuclear attack or a nuclear threat while the office of president is vacant. We should remind ourselves at this point that we did speak with the Commandant at the Judge

Advocate General School here in Charlottesville who told us, in implicit terms, that the Pentagon had already made provisions for a case in which the commander in chief (the president, vice president, Speaker of the House, president pro tem of the Senate, secretary of state, and all the way down the line) had been killed in a nuclear attack. In other words, what the Commandant was saying to us was that the military had every possible contingency already worked out. Nevertheless, our question still remains: Are those legal and binding contracts or legal and binding laws that the military has made, and if they are, who approved them? What Mr. Conrad suggests should be done if in fact we are worried about this problem is that we rewrite the Twenty-fifth Amendment in such a way that the chain not of political command or authority (the power to legislate, the power to veto, the power to sign executive orders, and so forth) but the power to control the U.S. Armed Forces be made very explicit and be put into law. In other words, what he suggests is that in a situation in which the office of the president is being contested, either because of an impeachment trial or because of an assassin's bullet or because of the invoking of the Twenty-fifth Amendment, that there be a mechanism (a constitutional mechanism) that would immediately turn over the chain of military command to a group composed of the U.S. Supreme Court, the Executive Branch and Congress, and that until such time as that crisis was resolved, the president (or presidents) be stripped of their military authority. As farfetched as this scenario sounds, we should remind ourselves that in Henry Kissinger's memoirs, he states that Alexander Haig, who was then Mr. Nixon's chief of staff, and Kissinger himself were debating whether or not to bring in the 82nd Airborne Division from Fort Bragg and have them surround the White House. Whether it was Mr. Nixon's, Mr. Haig's, or Mr. Kissinger's idea is irrelevant. The important fact is that in a crucial moment in our history when the power in the office of the presidency is being tested, there was at least the possibility that the White House was going to run like an armed camp in the military dictatorship. It should give us cause for thought.

11. Mr. Conrad is much more optimistic about the way the Twenty-fifth Amendment works than we are for a variety of reasons, one of which obviously is that he wrote the amendment so he has got to have some confidence in the way it would work. But another reason for his confidence, and one that we really overlooked, is that Mr. Conrad believes that today with the exposure the presidency gets in newspapers and magazines and over the electronic media, it is just about impossible for a president to hide behind a physical or mental illness. I, on the other hand, am a little more cynical about the role of the press because as you and I have seen, Mr. Roosevelt lied about his health and got away with it. Mr. Truman wasn't sick, but I have a feeling he could have gotten away with it. The only president that was forthcoming about his illness was Mr. Eisenhower, and his turned out to be a very transient illness. Mr. Kennedy lied about his illness and got away with it. Mr. Johnson to a certain extent lied about the effect of his heart attack. Certainly no one knew the condition of Mr. Nixon's mental state, and he got away with it. Mr. Ford had no illnesses as far as we know, neither did Mr. Carter, but now we are faced with the situation of Mr. Reagan and you and I have our grave doubts about the situation with him and certainly there has been nothing in the press, at least nothing that has been given much attention, to suggest that Mr. Reagan may not be fully competent at all times of the day to discharge his duties.

12. Mr. Conrad suggested that we do a couple of things before we go any further. One is that as a matter of courtesy we contact Senator Bayh and let him know what it is that we are doing. The second thing is that he said he would be willing to set up a conference with Senator Bayh, himself, you and me sometime in Washington (probably at the end of April) and put this all down on a tape recorder to be transcribed. He said he would do this under the stipulation that we paid for travel expenses and hotel in Washington, that we keep the transcripts out of the public eye until after the November election, and that we give him final editorial power over the transcripts. I

told him tentatively that all of those arrangements were acceptable to us and that I would be back in touch with him. I have since written him a letter thanking him for his interview and telling him that we would be in touch.

13. Finally, Mr. Conrad suggested that we have the following people serve on our commission. One is John Feerick, who is a young constitutional lawyer at New York University; also Paul Fruend, who is professor of law and medicine at Harvard Law School; himself, Larry Conrad, who is an attorney in Indianapolis; Griffin Bell, who was attorney general for Mr. Carter; Dean Rusk, former secretary of state under President Johnson; Sam Erwin, now retired but he was a senator from North Carolina and chaired the Watergate Committee hearings.

14. My own assessments are that Larry Conrad has a wealth of information to offer us, not only because he was so intimately involved in the writing of the Twenty-fifth Amendment (by the way, he also ghostwrote Birch Bayh's book, *One Heartbeat Away*), but because of the immense number of contacts that he has inside and outside of government. I think it would be good to cultivate his friendship and interest in this project and I think that either you or Ken Thompson or someone with a national reputation at the University might do well to make contact with him to let him know that in fact we are very serious about this. I changed my mind about him chairing the commission. Although he is very articulate and very knowledgeable, his interests right now are in the political field (he wants to get Walter Mondale elected president), and I am afraid of having someone with that vested an interest in a partisan political activity chairing this kind of a commission. Nevertheless, we might consider asking him to serve as a staff member.

CHAPTER ELEVEN

Memorandum from Research Assistant Lehman Ford to Dr. Kenneth Crispell on a Preliminary Meeting of the Presidential Disability Study Group*

The meeting of 12/14/84 was held to discuss plans for the future Presidential Disability Commission. In attendance were Dr. Kenneth R. Crispell (KRC), Professor Kenneth W. Thompson of the Miller Center, Professor Daniel Meador of the Law School, Dr. Julian Hartt, Wilson Newman, Staige Blackford, Palmer Weber, Lehman Ford (KRC's Research Assistant), and Reed Davis (Graduate Student at the Miller Center).

KRC began the discussion by describing the illnesses of Presidents Wilson, F. Roosevelt, Kennedy, and the heart condition of Winston Churchill. KRC said that his interests in presidential disability now include not only the medical issues (such as the physician/patient relationship), but also the constitutional ones, specifically *how* a vice president and Cabinet and, in the extreme case, Congress *determine* that a president is disabled pursuant to Section 4 of the Constitution's Twenty-fifth Amendment.

At this point the Reagan shooting was briefly discussed. KRC mentioned that the Marine colonel responsible for always having the nuclear football within the president's reach made it to the G.W.

---

*Memorandum of the 14 December 1984 meeting is printed with the permission of Dr. Kenneth R. Crispell.

Hospital emergency room, though it is still uncertain what exactly happened to him after that. KRC also described how White House Counsel Fred Fielding decided against implementing the Twenty-fifth Amendment, even though Reagan was "disabled" not only during the four-to-five hour operation to remove the bullet, but also during his approximately fortnight-long recovery. KRC told the participants that a good, hair-raising description of a mock nuclear-apocalypse jamboree can be found in the book *SIOP*.

Daniel Meador then discussed his conversations with Mary Lawton of the Justice Department's Office of Intelligence Review and Policy. Ms. Lawton stated that her office was studying the disability issue mostly in terms of nuclear attacks and not on health issues. She said that her staff was also studying whether the Constitution would permit vesting the vice president with the president's commander-in-chief powers since these are the target of the problem, so to speak.

In connection with the commander-in-chief issue, Palmer Weber reminded the participants that during Nixon's "final days" Secretary of Defense James Schlesinger had given instructions for no one to obey Nixon's orders as commander in chief. Weber suggested that the secretary's actions were arguably not a legitimate exercise within the command structure.

Kenneth Thompson then asked KRC whether the commission would be permitted to learn the secret military contingency plans for presidential inability/succession. KRC said that he and Carlos Gomez, co-author with KRC of *The Health of Heroes*, had unsuccessfully tried to elicit such information from the Army Judge Advocate General's Office. Palmer Weber suggested that the Commission would probably be astute enough to devise its own scenarios for discussion and would thus not have to try piercing the veil of classified data. Mr. Newman had been involved in the investigation of the Lockheed kickback scandals and said that even when he was privy to secret data, open discussion in any case had to be posed in the form of answers to anonymous, hypothetical questions.

The timetable for establishing the permanent commission was then discussed. Regarding a preliminary commission, Wilson Newman suggested that it could act as a "grand jury," setting the parameters for the discussion, which would then be done by the "petit jury"; that is, the permanent commission.

KRC said that full publicity would be possible after April 4th because (1) the Miller Center Board will have met, and (2) President Reagan's congressional honeymoon and its attendant publicity will have subsided. Professor Meador cautioned that publicity ought not to begin until all commission arrangements were final. Wilson Newman suggested inviting former presidents so that the commission might have a bipartisan patina.

Floor Show: The Arthur Miller Video on the Twenty-fifth Amendment

Professor Author Miller of Harvard Law School questioned various Washington eminentoes on implementation of the Twenty-fifth Amendment's disability provisions and the process for making the vice president acting president. In answer to one of Miller's legalistisch "hypoze," Lloyd Cutler, White House counsel during the Carter administration, said that he would not suggest invoking the amendment as a precautionary measure before the President visited Miller's hypothetical Third World country because such a practice, if made routine, could dilute the dramatic import of the Twenty-fifth Amendment and might insult Third World countries. Cutler said that if a terrorist attacked the President on an overseas junket and the news transmitted to Washington on the Chief's attack was incomplete, Washington would have to grapple with the Twenty-fifth Amendment's processes ad hoc (aka hip shooting).

Archibald Cox suggested executing a private agreement before chancy things like operations or trips to dangerous Third World countries, but Cutler reiterated that the Twenty-fifth Amendment should only be invoked for grave procedures. Former Senator Edmund Muskie seconded that motion. Jack Valenti, a Johnson courtier, said that when LBJ was at Bethesda Naval Hospital (for the gall bladder operation, I guess) the White House *staff* would have made the decision to implement the Twenty-fifth Amendment and reminded Miller that the "staff" is found nowhere in the Constitution.

Miller posed Hypo II: The president survived the terrorist attack but is subject to short but noticeable tune-outs. Miller asked Democratic party apparatchik Ann Lewis how she would react as a Cabinet member (secretary of the interior) to overtures on declaring the president disabled. Lewis astutely asserted that when the decisionmakers start sounding out the fringe members of the Cabinet, the goal isn't decision making but consolidating support; the decision has already been made.

The upshot of the group's thinking was that the vice president/Cabinet procedure sounds great in theory, but the "Unofficial Cabinet," that is, the White House staff, will be the real decisionmakers and in their zeal to protect the president *and* themselves, will probably be deterred from decisive action (per Cutler) even when the president's medical condition reaches the "critical" stage.

CHAPTER TWELVE

Memorandum to Paul Stephan from Daniel J. Meador on a Draft of the Twenty-fifth Amendment, Section 3*

I am leaving this memo in your box because I will be out of town on January 15 and 16 and thus probably would not have an opportunity to talk with you until next Monday. I gather that you will be back on hand before then, so I wanted to get this information to you in my absence.

Ken Thompson convened a meeting of Ken Crispell and me a few days ago. There seemed to be a generally favorable reaction to the draft you did on the Section 3 questions. I too think you did a good job, and I have only a few minor editorial suggestions and comments. At our meeting in your absence we agreed that we would like very much for you to review your draft in light of my comments and any other later thoughts you have and produce a revision that will then be sent to all commission members by the Miller Center.

Ken Crispell distributed to us a draft of some material he has done. I have not yet had a chance to read it. I assume that a copy has come to you. I suggest that it might be helpful for you to read this before you undertake a revision of your draft because there may be some points there you would want to take into account in your revision. We agreed at this meeting that it would be desirable

---

Memorandum of 14 January 1987 printed with the permission of Daniel J. Meador.

for the commission to attempt to formulate guidelines relating to the invocation of Section 3. My impression is that this is what Crispell has undertaken in his draft.

Attached is a copy of your draft that I have made editorial comments on. These are suggestions for alterations in wording that I submit simply for your consideration. In addition to these editorial suggestions, I offer the following comments.

The first heading—"Need for Change in the Law"—threw me off a bit at the outset. The heading suggests that you are going to discuss some proposed changes in the law and to make a case for a need for change. In fact, however, you come out with just the opposite conclusion. I'm wondering if some other heading might be desirable. I do not have a good suggestion in mind. What about something like "The Existing legal Framework"? Something like that would have a more neutral cast and would not suggest to the reader that there is a need or that we are going to argue for a change.

Your discussion of the constitutionality of a delegation by the president under Section 3 of his power to invoke that section leaves the matter more open than my taste would prefer. Personally, I would be more comfortable in coming down somewhat harder on the side of the unconstitutionality of such a delegation. I think we can say, quite accurately, that the question has not been definitively resolved. My own view is that Sections 3 and 4 provide the exclusive means for a transfer of presidential power. Either the president himself transfers the power under Section 3, or, if he is unable to do so, the vice president and Cabinet (or other body) jointly can transfer the power. It seems to me to be in line with accepted constitutional interpretation to say that when a provision in the Constitution provides as explicitly as these provisions do for a procedure, the prescribed procedure is the only one that can be followed. My hunch is that Birch Bayh would agree with this position. In short, my preference would be to take a clearer position in that direction in this draft. I can see all kinds of potential confusion and uncertainties that would arise if an attempted delegation under Section 3 were to be made and such delegated authority were to be exercised at a time when the president himself is unable to act. In the public interest, I believe that the commission should lean hard against such a line of thought.

At our meeting at the Miller Center it was reconfirmed that the commission will meet in Washington on Wednesday, January 28, although the time of day was not fixed. In Washington I had thought that it was agreed that the meeting would be in the afternoon (at the suggestion of Spong), but Ken Thompson said that Brownell was now talking about preferring a morning meeting. In any event, we will be informed of this when it is settled.

If you could attend promptly to revising your draft and getting the revision to Ken Thompson just as quickly as possible, I know that he would appreciate it, as he wants to make a mailing to commission members in the near future.

I will be back in my office on Monday, January 19, if you would like to talk to me.

APPENDIXES

Eisenhower-Nixon Agreement on Transfer of Power Dated 3 March 1958

Agreement made public on March 3, 1958:

1) In the event of inability the President would—if possible—so inform the Vice President, and the Vice President would serve as Acting President, exercising the powers and duties of the office until the inability had ended.

2) In the event of an inability which would prevent the President from so communicating with the Vice President, the Vice President, after such consultation as seems to him appropriate under the circumstances, would decide upon the devolution of the powers and duties of the office and would serve as Acting President until the disability had ended.

3) The President, in either event, would determine when the inability had ended and at that time would resume the full exercise of the powers and duties of the office.

Kennedy-Johnson Statement of Disability Agreement on Transfer of Power

Following is the text of the statement released by President Kennedy on 10 August 1961 (that late!) describing the disability agreement between him and Vice President Johnson that forms the basis for the new disability agreement between President Johnson and Vice President Humphrey:

Kennedy-Johnson Statement.

The President and the Vice President have agreed to adhere to procedures identical to those which former President Eisenhower and Vice President Nixon adopted with regard to any questions of Presidential inability. Those procedures are as follows:

1) In the event if inability the President would—if possible—so inform the Vice President, and the Vice President would serve as Acting President, exercising the powers and duties of the office until the inability had ended.

2) In the event of an inability which would prevent the President from so communicating with the Vice President, the Vice President, after such consultation as seems to him appropriate under the circumstances, would decide on the devolution of the powers and duties of the

office and would serve as Acting President until the inability had ended.

3) The President, in either event, would determine when the inability had ended and at that time would resume the full exercise of the powers and duties of the office.

After consultation with the Attorney General, it is the understanding of the President and the Vice President that these procedures reflect the correct interpretations to be given to Article II, Section 1, Clause 5 of the Constitution. This was also the view of the prior Administration and is supported by the great majority of constitutional scholars.

The relevant constitutional provision is:

> In the case of the removal of the President from office, or of his death, resignation, or inability to discharge the powers and duties of the said office, the same shall devolve on the Vice President, and the Congress may be law provide for the case of removal, death, resignation, or inability, both of the President and Vice President, declaring what officers shall then act as President, and such officers shall act accordingly, until the disability be removed, or a President shall be elected.

Under this provision, upon a proper determination of Presidential inability, the Vice President succeeds temporarily to the powers and duties of the Presidency until such times as the President is enabled to act again. Unlike the case of removal, death, or resignation, the Vice President does not permanently become President.

Under the arrangement quoted above, the Vice President agrees to serve as Acting President "after such consultations as seems to him appropriate under the circumstances." There is no provision of the Constitution or of law prescribing any procedure of consultation, but the President and Vice President felt, as a matter of wisdom and sound judgment, that the Vice President would wish to have the support of the Cabinet as to the necessity and desirability of discharging the powers and duties of the Presidency as

Acting President as well as legal advice from the Attorney General that the circumstances would, under the Constitution, justify his doing so. The understanding between the President and the Vice President authorizes the Vice President to consult with these officials with a free mind that this is what the President intended in the event of a crisis.

Prior to the Eisenhower-Nixon arrangement, there were no similar understandings of a public nature. For this reason Vice Presidents have hesitated to take any initiative during the period when the President was disabled. Obviously, this is a risk which cannot be taken in these times, and it is for that reason that President Kennedy and Vice President Johnson have agreed to follow the precedent established by the past Administration.

Letter from President Reagan and Excerpted Column on Transfer of Power

TEXT OF THE PRESIDENT'S LETTER

BETHESDA, Md., July 13 (AP)—Following is the text of President Reagan's letter to the President pro tempore of the Senate and the Speaker of the House notifying them that Vice President Bush would temporarily discharge the powers and duties of the President:

I am about to undergo surgery during which time I will be briefly and temporarily incapable of discharging the constitutional powers and duties of the office of the President of the United States.

After consultation with my counsel and the Attorney General, I am mindful of the provisions of Section 3 of the 25th Amendment to the Constitution and of the uncertainties of its application to such brief and temporary periods of incapacity. I do not believe that the drafters of this amendment intended its application to situations such as the instant one.

Nevertheless, consistent with my longstanding arrangement with Vice President George Bush, and not intending to set a precedent binding anyone privileged to hold the office in the future, I have determined and it is my intention and direction, that Vice President George Bush shall discharge those powers and duties in my stead commencing with the administration of anesthesia to me in this instance.

I shall advise you and the Vice President when I determine that I am able to resume the discharge of the constitutional powers and duties of this office.

May God bless this nation and us all.

Sincerely,
Ronald Reagan

ON TRANSFERRING POWER

After President Reagan underwent surgery to remove an assassin's bullet on March 30, 1981, some members of Congress criticized Administration officials for not invoking the 25th Amendment. On the morning of July 13, as the White House was saying that Vice President Bush's return from his home in Maine to Washington was unrelated to the President's unexpected abdominal surgery, Mr. Reagan was choosing between two letters. One formally invoked 25th Amendment procedures for voluntary transfer of constitutional power to the Vice President in a time of Presidential incapacity. The other delegated power but cast doubt on the Amendment's applicability to the situation. Mr. Reagan selected the latter, White House officials later said, in part because he did not want to set a precedent creating pressure for Presidents to yield their powers whenever briefly sedated. But, legal experts agree, Mr. Bush was Acting President for eight hours. It was the first Presidential action to conform to the Amendment's requirements for notification of Congress. The Amendment was inspired by the ambiguity over exactly when Vice President Johnson became President after President Kennedy was shot. Orderly transfer matters, White House officials said, to make it clear who is in command of the armed forces.

Excerpt on the Twenty-fifth Amendment from *Barbara Bush: A Memoir**

Soon after taking office George called a meeting in the Oval Office that included the Vice President; Boyden Gray, a trusted friend and George's chief counsel for twelve years; the Chief of Staff, John Sununu; Burt Lee, good friend and the President's doctor; Susan Porter Rose; and myself. The purpose of the gathering was to discuss the Twenty-fifth Amendment to the Constitution: what would happen if George got ill, what the law was, and what we all should do. It is a dreadful thought, but one every president must think about and face. George led the discussion, and I remember two things very clearly: Dan Quayle sitting quietly, saying not a word; he was in a most sensitive position. And Burt Lee saying that the people in that room would be the most likely to notice a change if George were ill and must be ready to declare him unable to continue to be in charge. What an awful burden for a friend—not to mention a spouse. I am glad that we never had to face that issue. I think George wanted this meeting early on so that the performance of the Wilson administration would not be repeated, when the President's illness had been hidden from the public for months. We all promised George that we would be honest and responsible, no matter how hard. Boyden explained the

---

Reprinted from Barbara Bush: A Memoir *(New York: Charles Scribner's Sons, 1994), 282.*

legal side to us. That settled, we decided that we would never talk about this meeting since any discussion about the president's health starts rumors.